HIGH VOICE

ART SONG IN ENGLISH

50 SONGS BY 21 AMERICAN AND BRITISH COMPOSERS

EDITED BY CAROL KIMBALL

BOOSEY & HAWKES

DISTRIBUTED BY

7777 W. BLUEMOUND RD. P.O. BOX 13819 MILWAUKEE, WI 53213

For all works contained herein:
Unauthorized copying, arranging, adapting, recording or public performance is an infringement of copyright.
Infringers are liable under the law.

www.boosey.com
www.halleonard.com

PREFACE

Bright is the ring of words
When the right man rings them,
Fair the fall of songs
When the singer sings them.
    — Robert Louis Stevenson

Art Song in English is eclectic in content. The fifty songs in this collection were purposely chosen as being "singer-friendly" and varied in style, linked by the common bond of the English language. As the collection took shape, a "sampler" of American and British songs emerged. It also became quite clear that the first part of the twentieth century was an important and productive era in the development of art song in both countries. Many of these composers' lives intertwined as teachers, students, colleagues, and friends. Viewed as a whole, their work forms the backbone of American and British song literature.

Choosing fifty songs was a difficult task. Fortunately, Boosey & Hawkes has a long and distinguished tradition of publishing vocal music in English, and their extensive catalog offered many varied choices. We wanted songs that teachers and students would find useful in the studio and in recital, representing a broad survey of song literature. This collection provides a substantial introduction to twentieth century American and British art song, combining familiar repertoire with less well known but nonetheless important examples of song. Although there are a few gender-specific texts, care was taken to make the volume useful for all voices.

The composers in this collection were attracted by poetry of the highest quality, a multi-hued patchwork of words and ideas. Some of the most familiar names in English language verse are represented here, a veritable "who's-who" of poets spanning more than four centuries, including, among others, William Shakespeare; W.B. Yeats; Robert Frost; Emily Dickinson; A.E. Housman; Robert Louis Stevenson; e.e. cummings; Walt Whitman; John Masefield; and Christina Rossetti.

The texts offer a kaleidoscope of dramatic situations and emotional states in musical settings. Rebecca Clarke's chilling "The Seal Man"; Ivor Gurney's masterpiece "Sleep"; Jack Beeson's contemporary transformation of the Viennese waltz, "In the Public Gardens"; Michael Head's vigorous "Money, O!"; Arthur Somervell's "The lads in their hundreds", its deeply-felt setting tinged with the colors of the English countryside; Ned Rorem's exciting and rhythmically charged "Alleluia"; Richard Hundley's gently evocative "The Astronomers"; Gerald Finzi's majestic "Fear no more the heat o' the sun"; and Leonard Bernstein's manic recipe "Rabbit at Top Speed" are only a partial listing of the treasury of colorful scenes and situations found in this collection.

There are a number of folk song arrangements included in this collection, but arrangement seems an unfair description. These are fully-composed art song treatments of folk songs, designed for the recital stage, akin to art song by any reasonable viewpoint. Ned Rorem's artful setting of Stephen Foster's "Jeanie with the Light Brown Hair" is in the same spirit, with new and evocative harmonic textures.

Each song sings with the unique voice of its composer, its lyricism forged by the composer's sensitive approaches to text and extraordinary warmth of feeling for the human voice. These art songs deserve to be studied and performed.

Carol Kimball
Editor
August, 2006

CONTENTS

DOMINICK ARGENTO
- 12 Dirge
- 8 Spring
- 22 Spring is like a perhaps hand
- 15 when faces called flowers float out of the ground

JACK BEESON
- 24 In the Public Gardens
- 29 Indiana Homecoming

LEONARD BERNSTEIN
- 34 Civet à Toute Vitesse (Rabbit at Top Speed)
- 32 Greeting
- 39 I hate music!
- 42 Jupiter has seven moons

FRANK BRIDGE
- 46 Love went a-riding

BENJAMIN BRITTEN
- 63 At the mid hour of night
- 60 If it's ever spring again
- 52 Nocturne
- 66 The Salley Gardens
- 56 Sephestia's Lullaby

THEODORE CHANLER
- 69 These, My Ophelia

REBECCA CLARKE
- 80 Down by the salley gardens
- 72 The Seal Man

AARON COPLAND
- 90 At the River
- 86 Heart, we will forget him
- 93 The Little Horses
- 88 Poet's Song
- 83 Why do they shut me out of Heaven?

DAVID DEL TREDICI
- 96 Acrostic Song

JOHN DUKE
- 102 Central Park at Dusk
- 104 There will be stars

GERALD FINZI
110 Fear no more the heat o' the sun
115 It was a lover and his lass
124 Oh fair to see

CARLISLE FLOYD
Two Stevenson Songs:
126   Rain
127   Where Go the Boats?

IVOR GURNEY
130 Sleep

MICHAEL HEAD
134 Money, O!

RICHARD HUNDLEY
138 The Astronomers
140 Sweet Suffolk Owl
142 Waterbird

JOHN IRELAND
107 Spring Sorrow

ROGER QUILTER
148 How should I your true love know?
154 My Life's Delight
151 Weep you no more

NED ROREM
158 Alleluia
162 Ferry me across the water
164 Jeanie with the Light Brown Hair
168 Love
171 Stopping by Woods on a Snowy Evening

ARTHUR SOMERVELL
174 The lads in their hundreds

RALPH VAUGHAN WILLIAMS
182 Bright is the ring of words
185 Linden Lea

PETER WARLOCK
180 Take, O take those lips away

POET INDEX

ANONYMOUS
158 Alleluia
138 The Astronomers
90 At the River
93 The Little Horses
140 Sweet Suffolk Owl
151 Weep you no more

W.H. AUDEN
52 Nocturne

WILLIAM BARNES
185 Linden Lea

JOHN BETJEMAN
24 In the Public Gardens

LEONARD BERNSTEIN
32 Greeting
39 I hate music!
42 Jupiter has seven moons

RUPERT BROOKE
107 Spring Sorrow

THOMAS CAMPION
154 My Life's Delight

LEWIS CARROLL
96 Acrostic Song

MARY E. COLERIDGE
46 Love went a-riding

E.E. CUMMINGS
88 Poet's Song
22 Spring is like a perhaps hand
15 when faces called flowers float out of the ground

W.H. DAVIES
134 Money, O!

EMILY DICKINSON
86 Heart, we will forget him
83 Why do they shut me out of Heaven?

ÉMILE DUMONT
34 Civet à Toute Vitesse (trans. Bernstein)

JOHN FLETCHER
130 Sleep

STEPHEN FOSTER
164 Jeanie with the Light Brown Hair

ROBERT FROST
171 Stopping by Woods on a Snowy Evening

ROBERT GREENE
56 Sephestia's Lullaby

THOMAS HARDY
60 If it's ever spring again

A.E. HOUSMAN
174 The lads in their hundreds

ABRAHAM LINCOLN (adapted)
29 Indiana Homecoming

THOMAS LODGE
168 Love

ARCHIBALD MACLEISH
69 These, My Ophelia

JOHN MASEFIELD
72 The Seal Man

THOMAS MOORE
63 At the mid hour of night

THOMAS NASH
8 Spring

JAMES PURDY
142 Waterbird

CHRISTINA ROSSETTI
162 Ferry me across the water
124 Oh fair to see

WILLIAM SHAKESPEARE
12 Dirge
110 Fear no more the heat o' the sun
148 How should I your true love know?
115 It was a lover and his lass
180 Take, O take those lips away

ROBERT LOUIS STEVENSON
182 Bright is the ring of words
126 Rain
127 Where Go the Boats?

SARA TEASDALE
102 Central Park at Dusk
104 There will be stars

W.B. YEATS
80 Down by the salley gardens
66 The Salley Gardens

for Nicholas Di Virgilio

Spring

from *Six Elizabethan Songs*
original key

THOMAS NASH

DOMINICK ARGENTO

© Copyright 1970 by Boosey & Hawkes, Inc. Copyright Renewed.
Copyright for all countries. All rights reserved.

Dirge

for Nicholas Di Virgilio

from *Six Elizabethan Songs*

original key

WILLIAM SHAKESPEARE
DOMINICK ARGENTO

© Copyright 1970 by Boosey & Hawkes, Inc. Copyright Renewed.
Copyright for all countries. All rights reserved.

when faces called flowers float out of the ground

from *Songs about Spring*
original key

e.e. cummings

DOMINICK ARGENTO

© Copyright 1980 by Boosey & Hawkes, Inc. Copyright Renewed.
Text: © Copyright 1923, 1925, 1949, 1951 by e.e. cummings
Reprinted by permission of Harcourt, Brace & Jovanovich, Inc.
Copyright for all countries. All rights reserved.

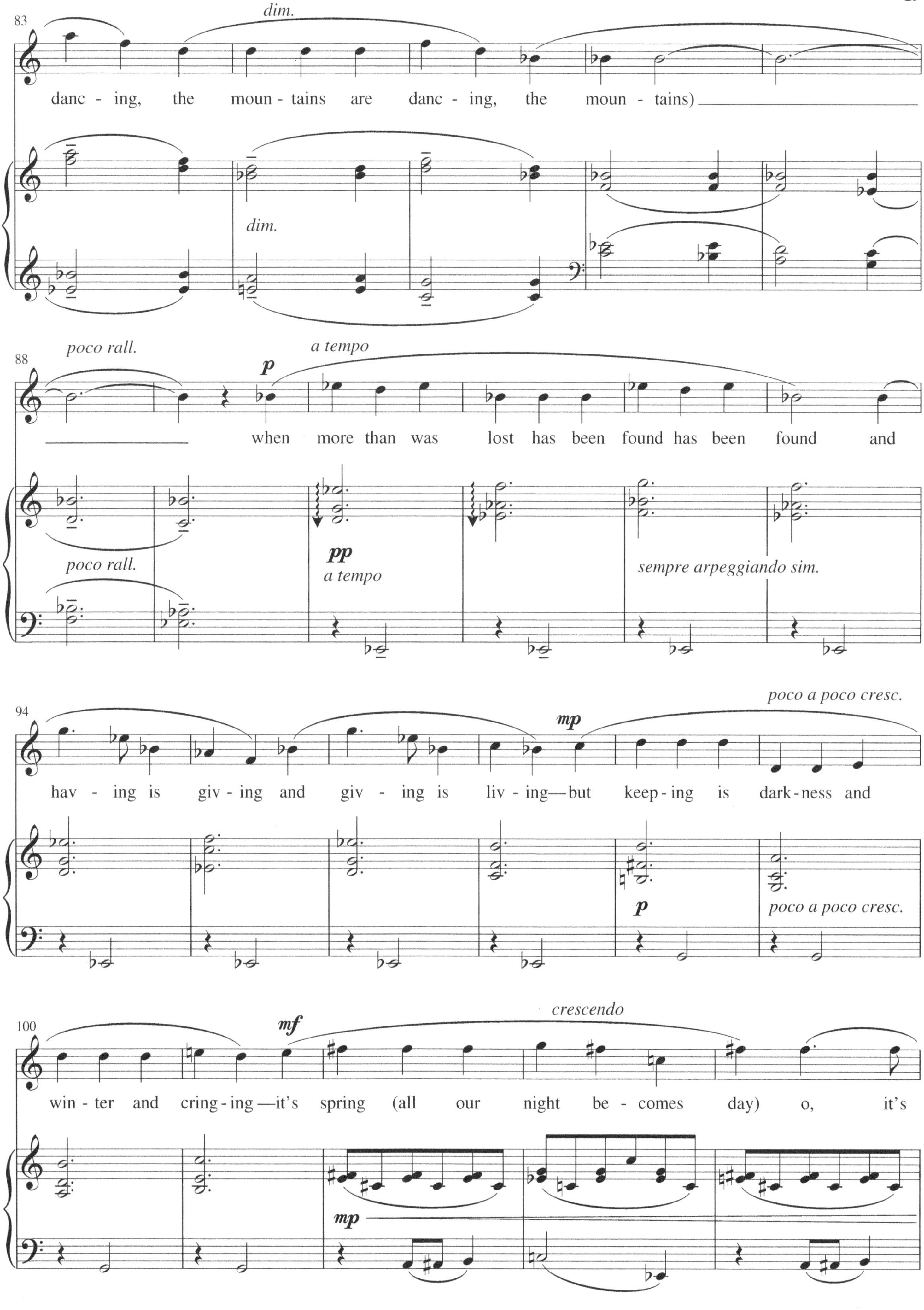
83
dim.
danc - ing, the moun - tains are danc - ing, the moun - tains)
dim.
88
poco rall.
a tempo
p
when more than was lost has been found has been found and
poco rall.
pp
a tempo
sempre arpeggiando sim.
94
poco a poco cresc.
mp
hav - ing is giv - ing and giv - ing is liv - ing—but keep - ing is dark - ness and
p
poco a poco cresc.
100
crescendo
mf
win - ter and cring - ing—it's spring (all our night be - comes day) o, it's
mp

In the Public Gardens
original key

JOHN BETJEMAN

JACK BEESON

Text: © Copyright Estate of John Betjeman.
Used by permission.
© Copyright 2003 by Boosey & Hawkes, Inc.
Copyright for all countries. All rights reserved.

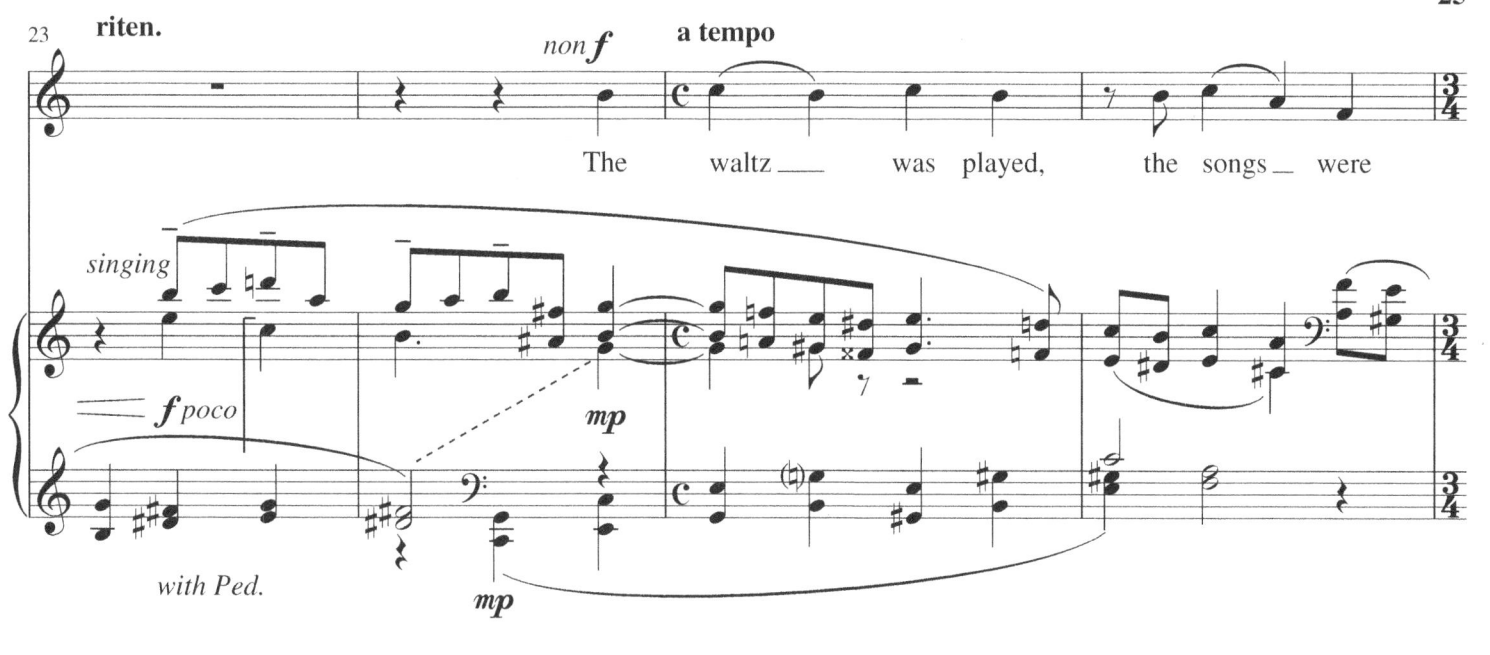

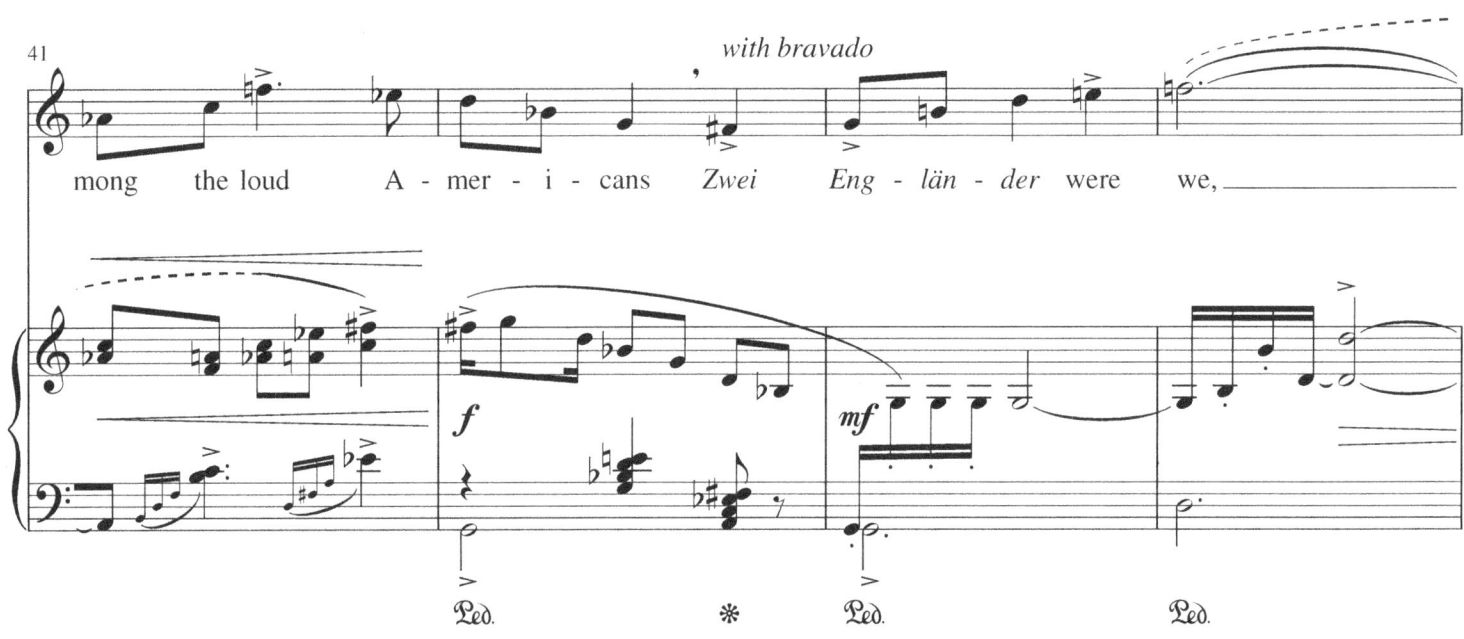
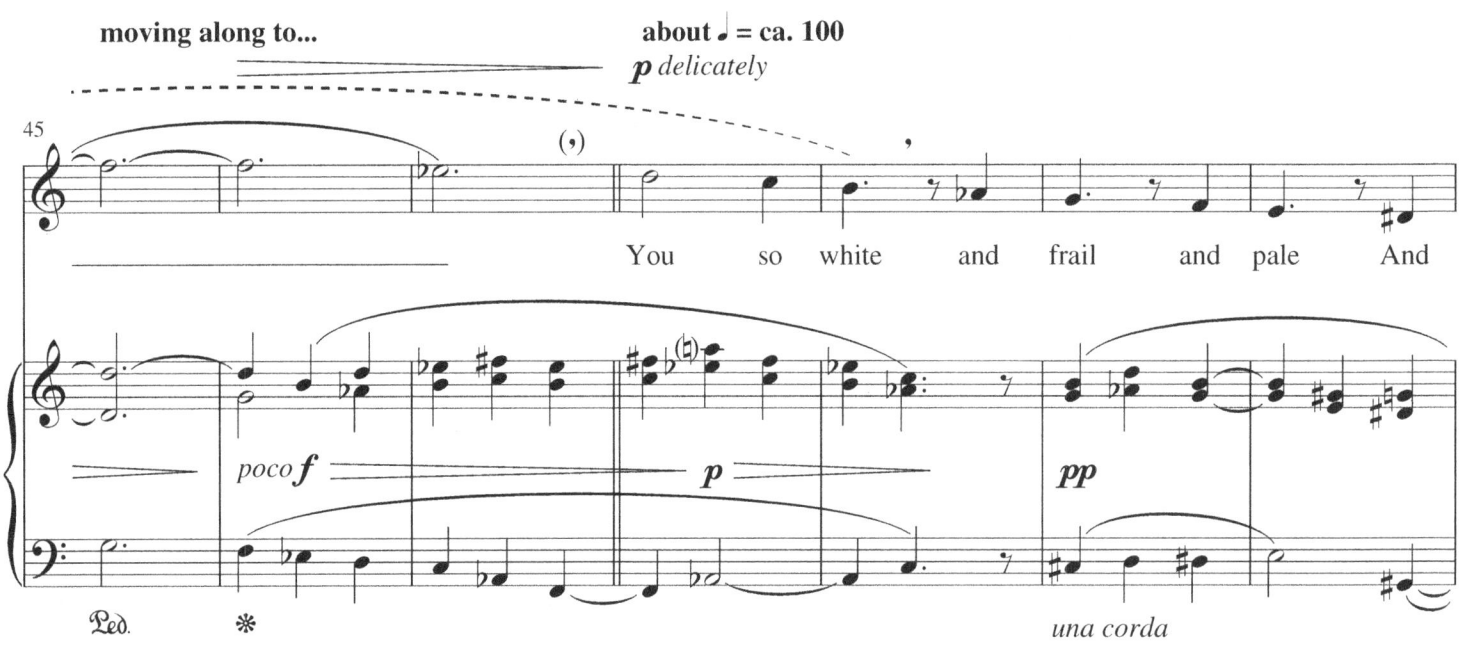

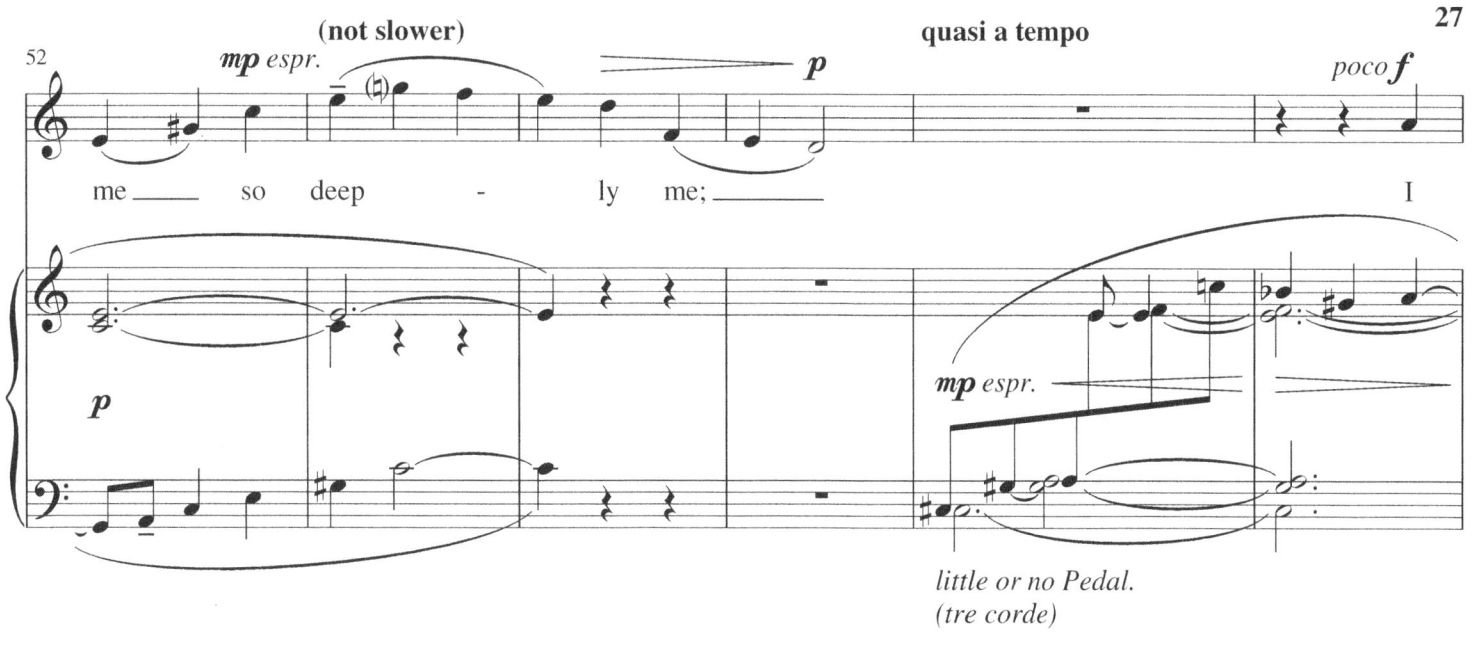

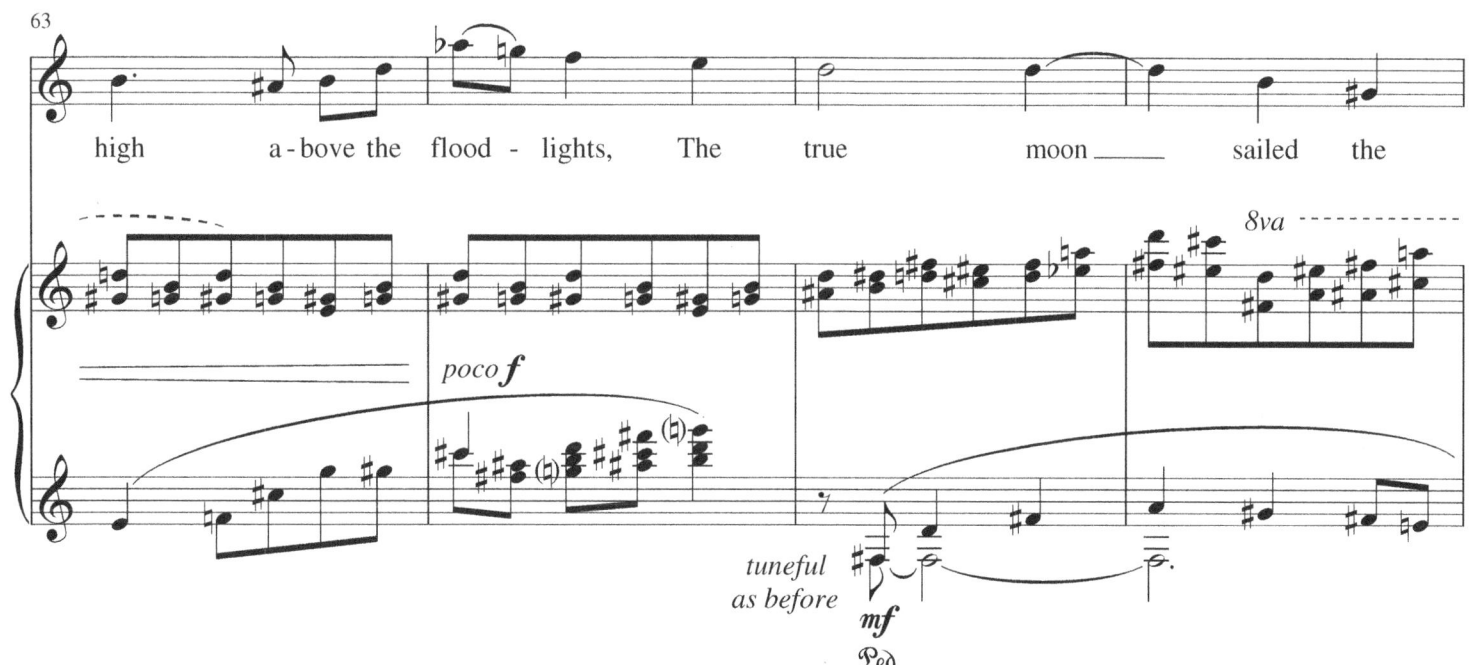

Indiana Homecoming

original key for Baritone or Bass-Baritone: a minor 3rd lower

ABRAHAM LINCOLN
(adapted)

JACK BEESON

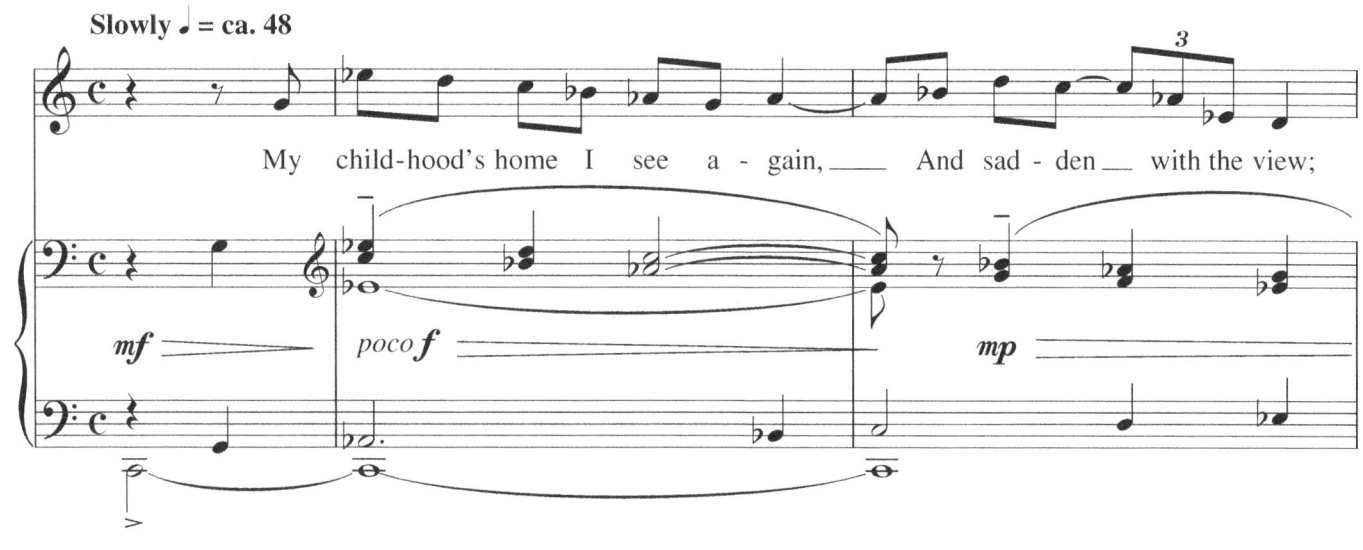

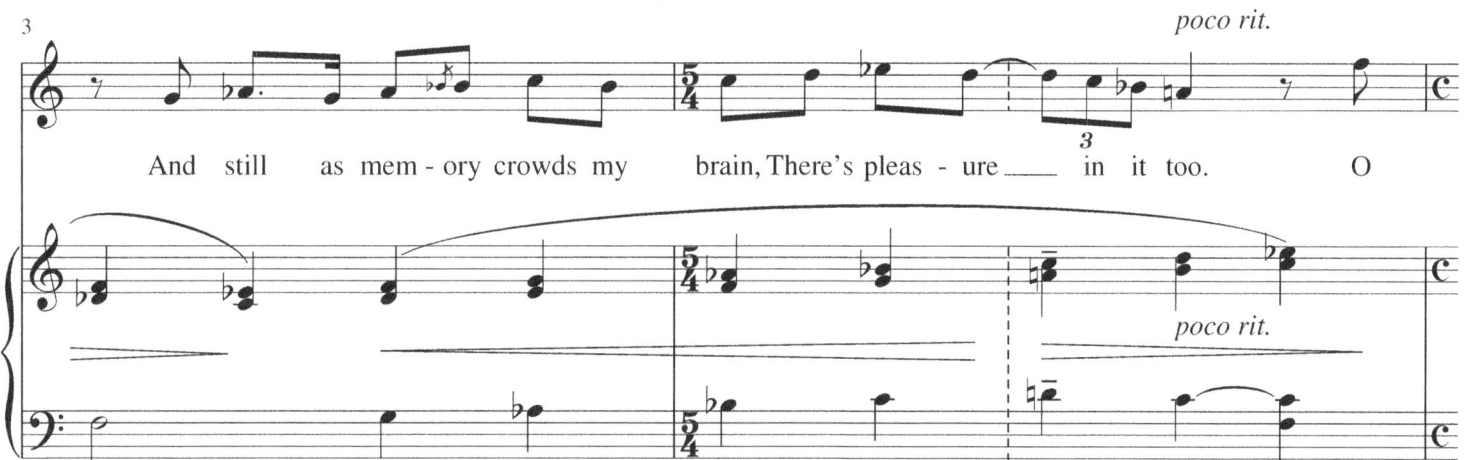

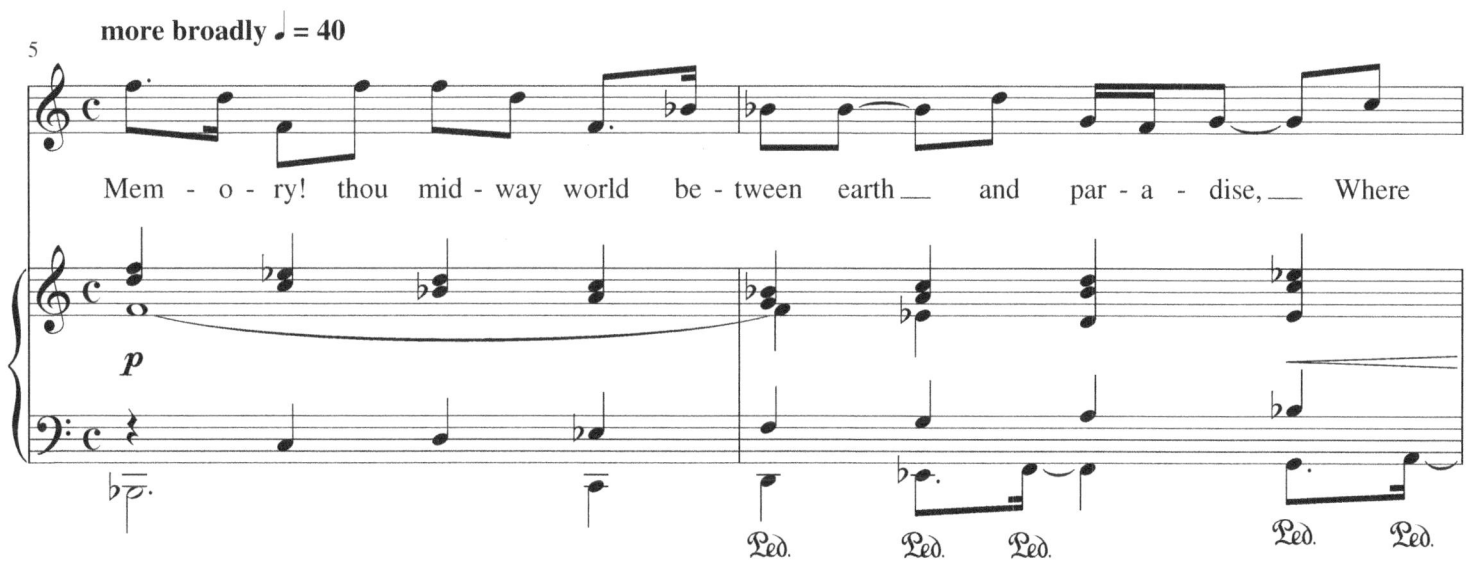

© Copyright 1973 by Boosey & Hawkes, Inc.
New transposition © 2006 by Boosey & Hawkes, Inc.
Copyright for all countries. All rights reserved.

December, 1956; N.Y.C.

for J.G.

Greeting
from *Arias and Barcarolles*
original key: a minor 3rd lower

Words and Music by
LEONARD BERNSTEIN

Civet à Toute Vitesse

(Rabbit at Top Speed)

from *La Bonne Cuisine (Four Recipes)*

original key: a major 2nd lower

Texts from "La Bonne Cuisine Française"
by ÉMILE DUMONT
English version by L. B.

LEONARD BERNSTEIN

© Copyright 1949 by The Estate of Leonard Bernstein. Copyright Renewed.
New transposition © 2006 by Boosey & Hawkes, Inc.
Leonard Bernstein Music Publishing Company LLC, Publisher.
Boosey & Hawkes, Inc., Sole Agent.

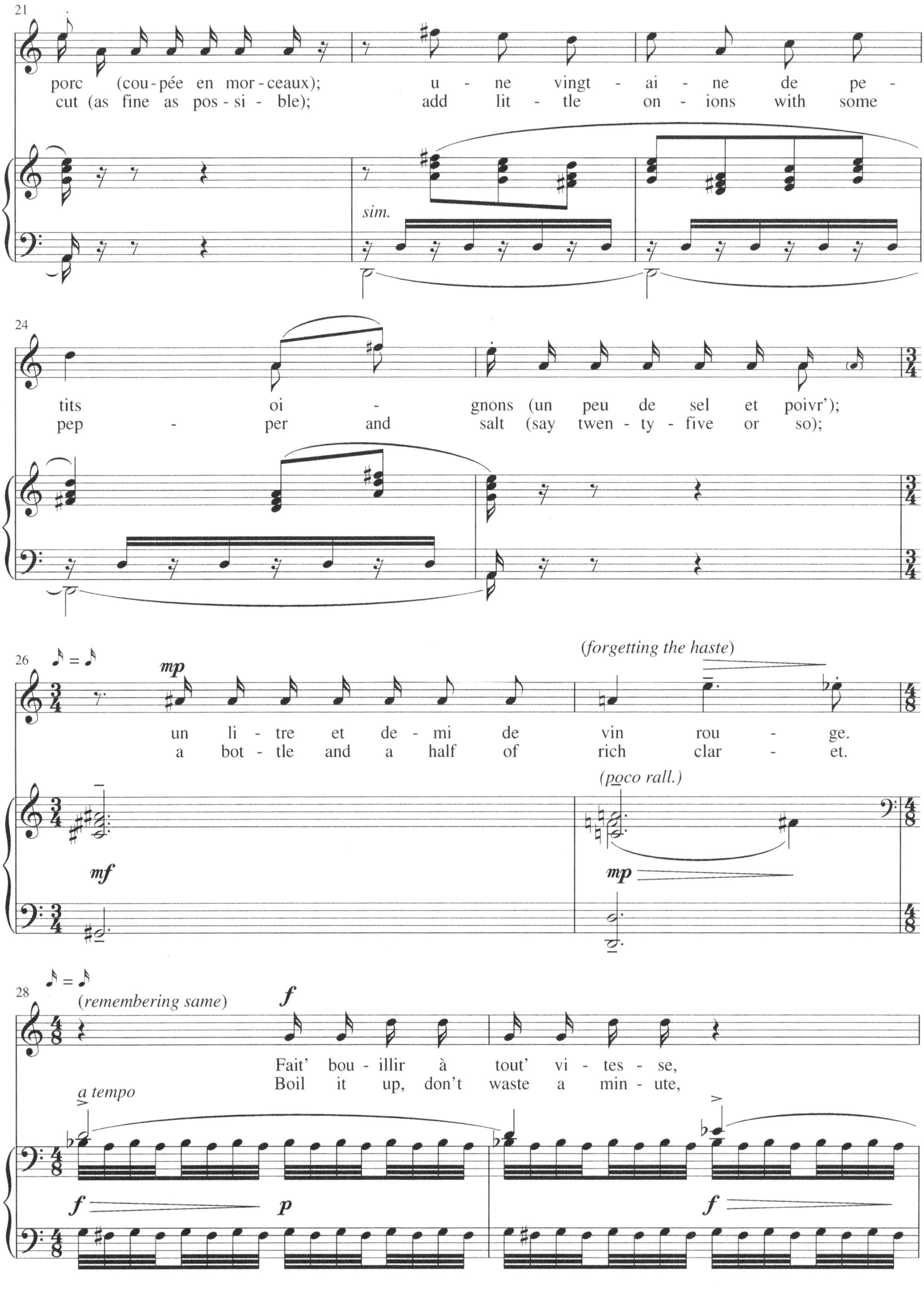
porc (cou-pée en mor-ceaux); u - ne vingt - ai - ne de pe -
cut (as fine as pos-si - ble); add lit - tle on - ions with some
sim.
tits oi - gnons (un peu de sel et poivr');
pep - per and salt (say twen - ty - five or so);
(forgetting the haste)
mp
un li - tre et de - mi de vin rou - ge.
a bot - tle and a half of rich clar - et.
(poco rall.)
mf
mp
(remembering same)
f
Fait' bou - illir à tout' vi - tes - se,
Boil it up, don't waste a min - ute,
a tempo
f
p
f

I hate music!

from *I Hate Music!*
original key

Words and Music by
LEONARD BERNSTEIN

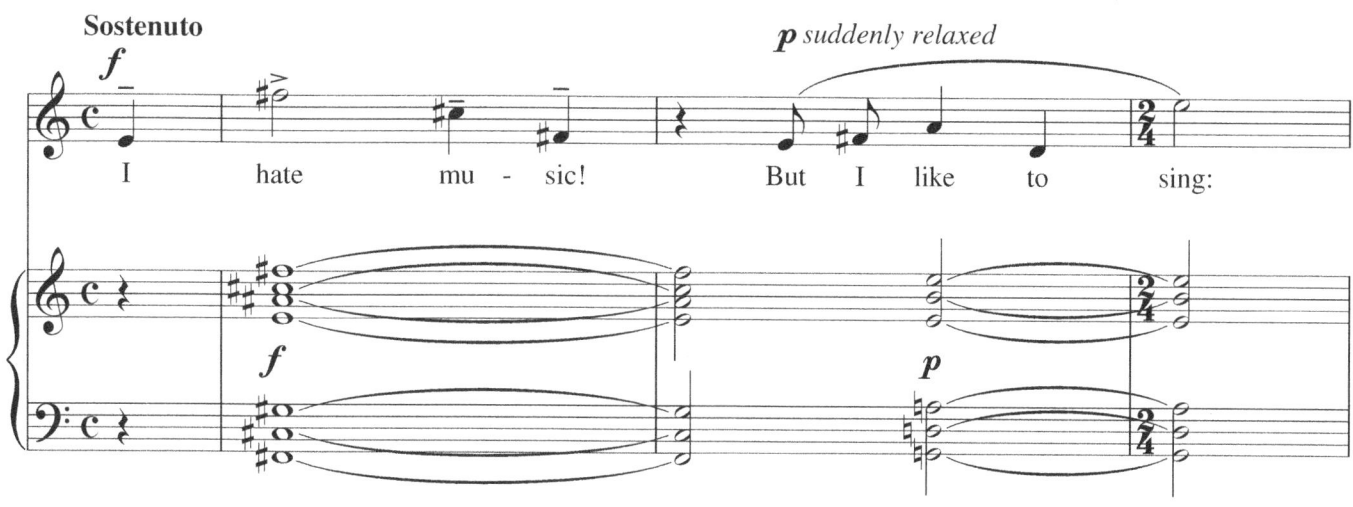
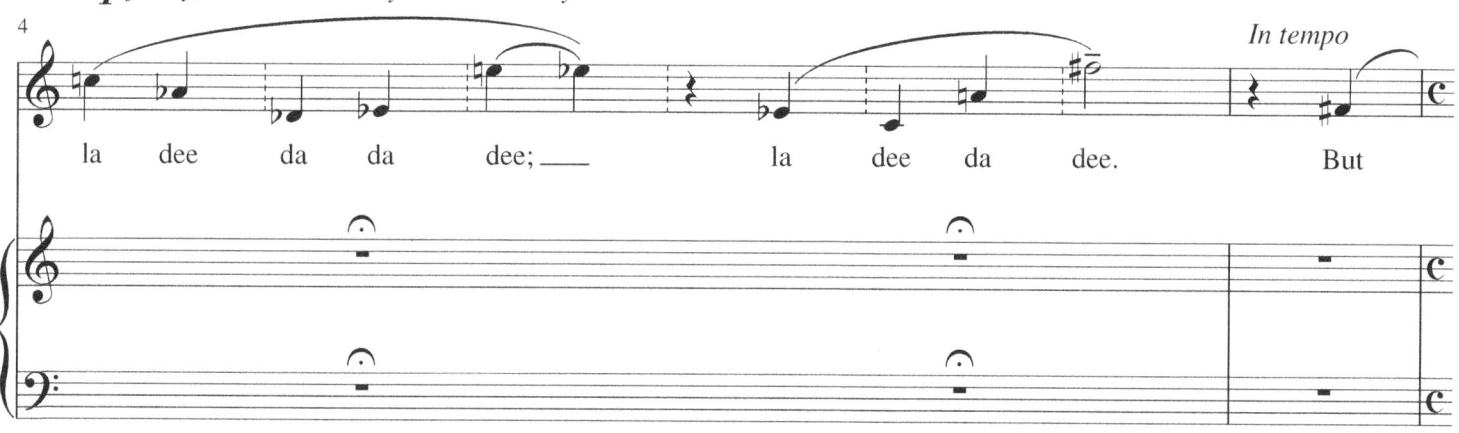

© Copyright 1943 by M. Witmark & Sons. Copyright Renewed by Warner Bros. Inc.
Leonard Bernstein Music Publishing Company LLC, Publisher.
Boosey & Hawkes, Inc., Sole Agent.

42

Jupiter has seven moons

from *I Hate Music!*
original key

Words and Music by
LEONARD BERNSTEIN

© Copyright 1943 by M. Witmark & Sons. Copyright Renewed by Warner Bros. Inc.
Leonard Bernstein Music Publishing Company LLC, Publisher.
Boosey & Hawkes, Inc., Sole Agent.

Love went a-riding
original key

MARY E. COLERIDGE

FRANK BRIDGE

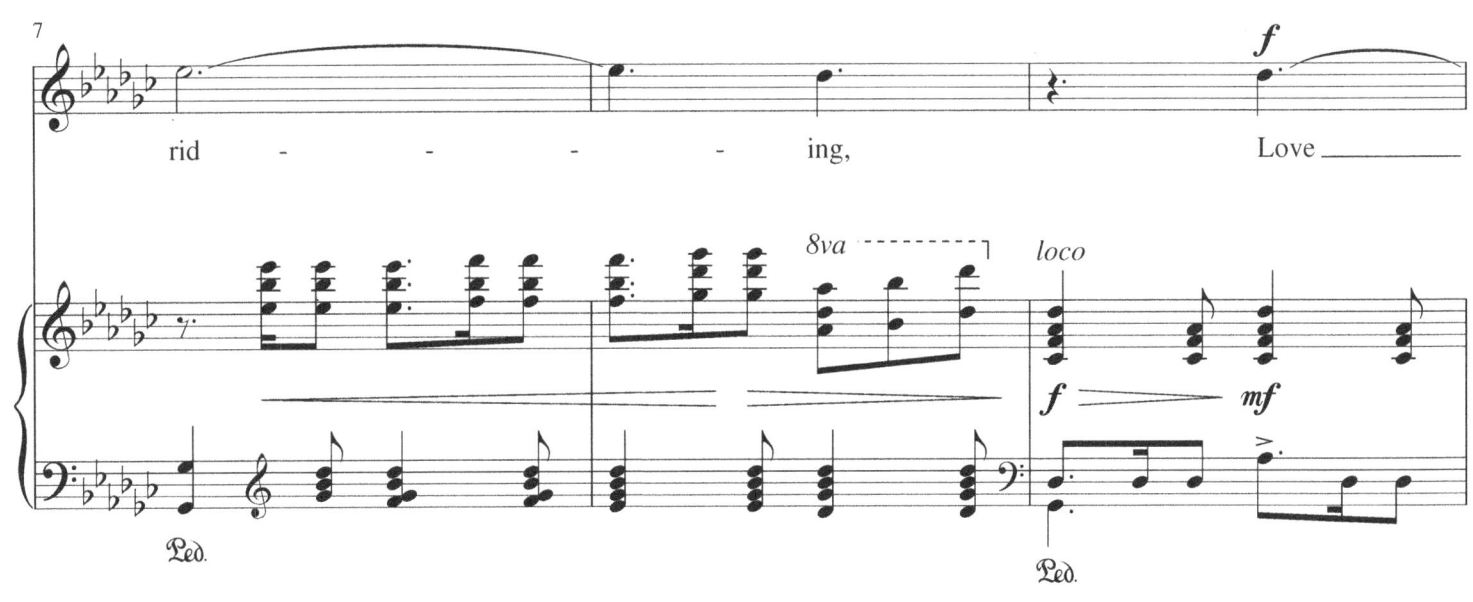

© Copyright 1916, by Winthrop Rogers Ltd.
All rights reserved

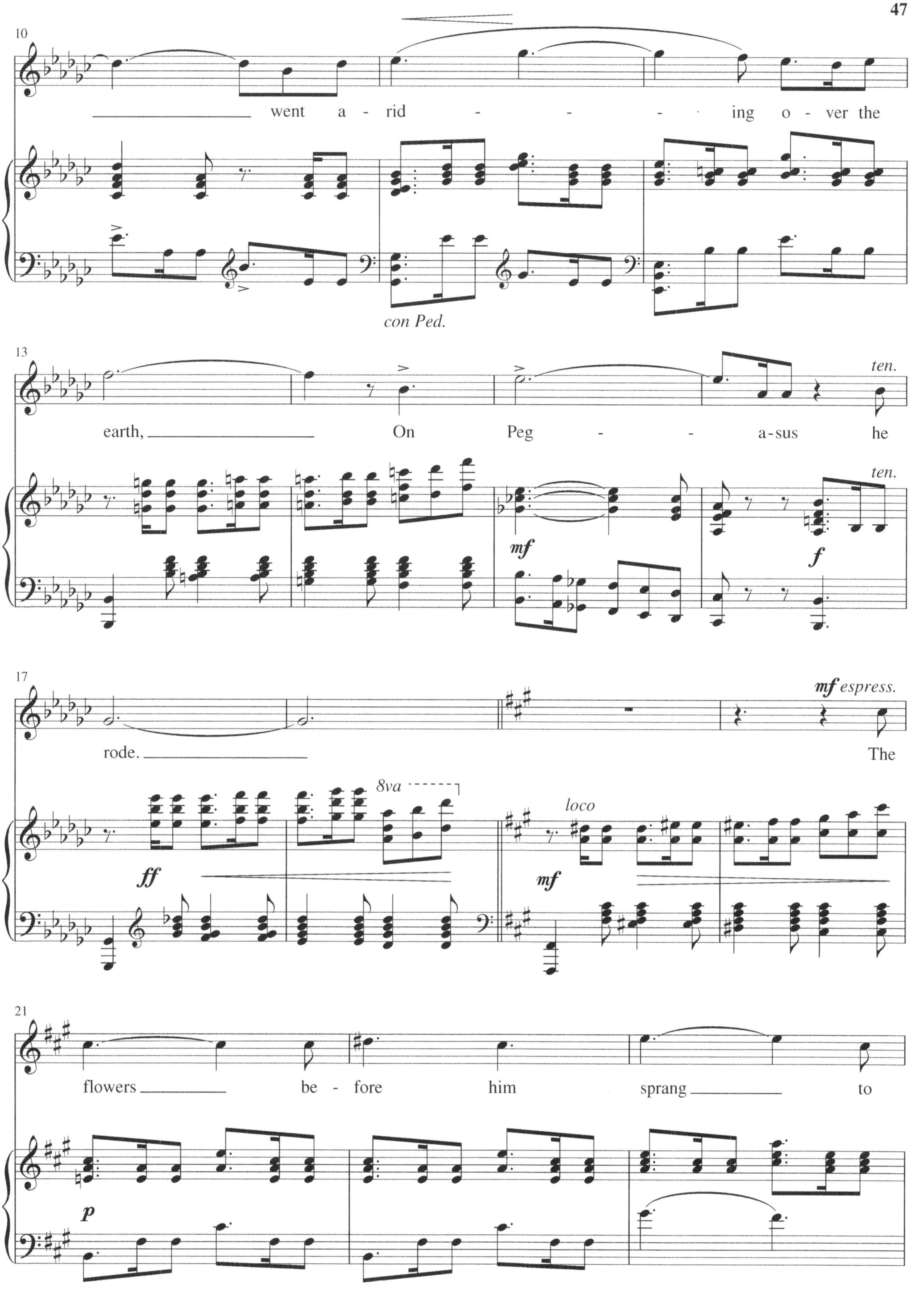
10
went a - rid - - - ing o - ver the
con Ped.
13
earth, On Peg - - a-sus he
ten.
mf
f
17
rode. The
mf espress.
8va
loco
ff
mf
21
flowers be - fore him sprang to
p

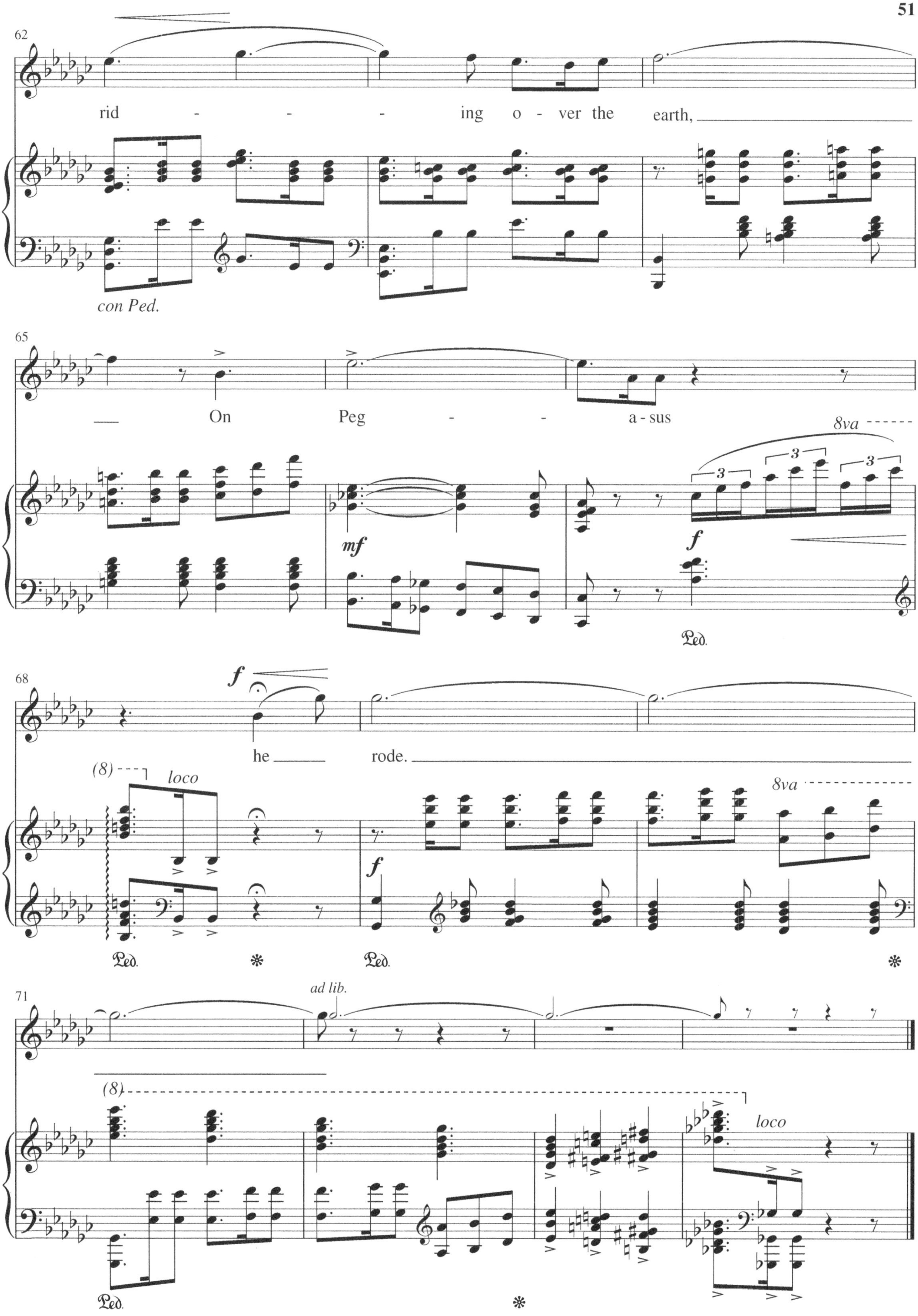
62
rid - - - ing o - ver the earth,
con Ped.
65
On Peg - - a - sus
mf
f
8va
Ped.
68
f
he rode.
(8)
loco
f
8va
Ped.
71
ad lib.
(8)
loco
Ped.

Nocturne

from *On This Island*
original key

W.H. AUDEN

BENJAMIN BRITTEN

WINTHROP ROGERS EDITION
Copyright 1938 by Boosey & Co. Ltd. Copyright Renewed.
All rights reserved

Sephestia's Lullaby

from *A Charm of Lullabies*
original key: a minor 3rd lower

ROBERT GREENE

BENJAMIN BRITTEN

© Copyright 1949 by Boosey & Co. Ltd. Copyright Renewed.
New transposition © 2006 by Boosey & Hawkes Music Publishers Ltd.
Copyright for all countries
All rights reserved

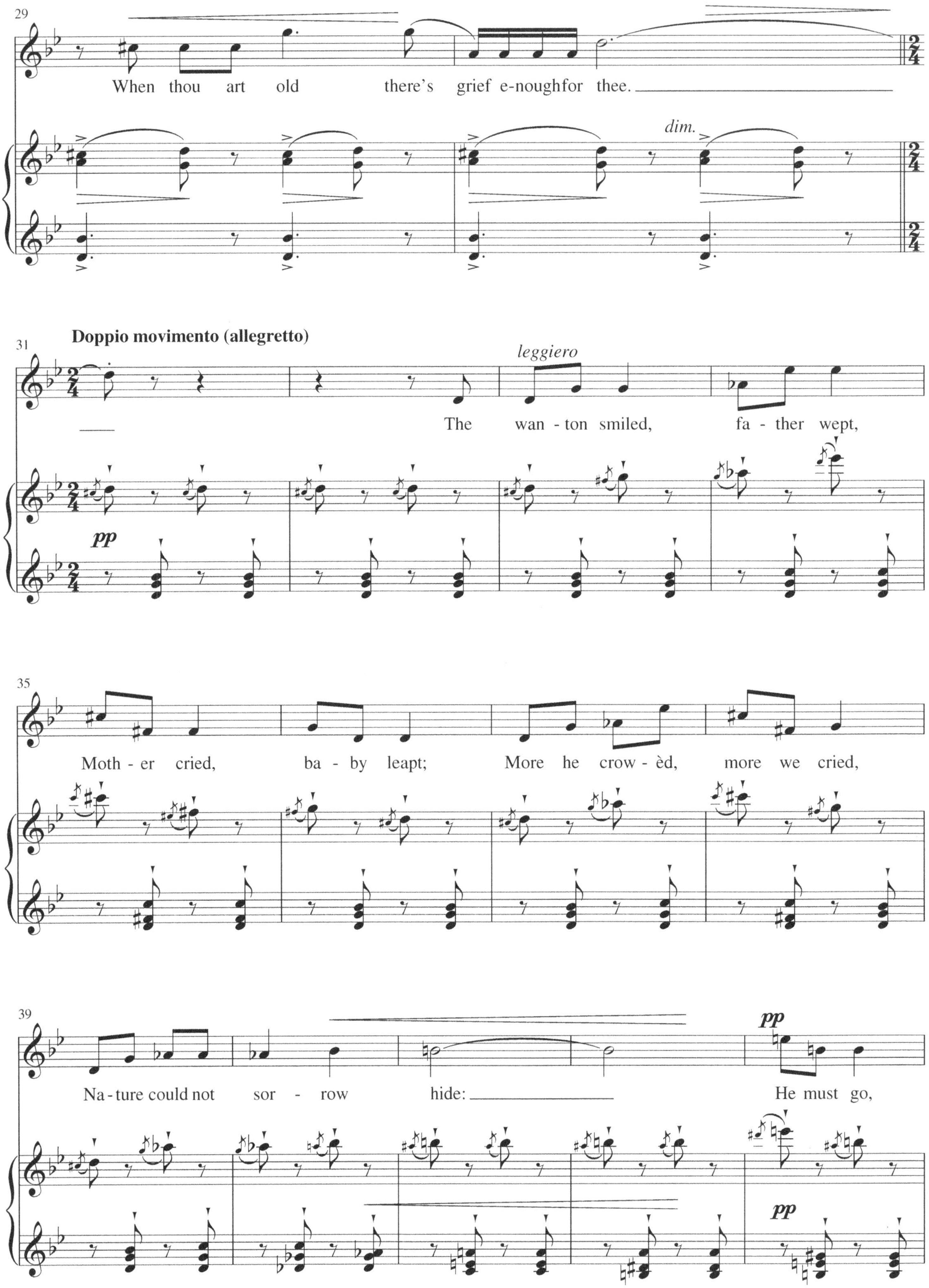
29
When thou art old there's grief e-nough for thee.
dim.
31
Doppio movimento (allegretto)
leggiero
The wan - ton smiled, fa - ther wept,
pp
35
Moth - er cried, ba - by leapt;
More he crow - èd, more we cried,
39
Na - ture could not sor - row hide:
pp
He must go,
pp

If it's ever spring again

cut from *Winter Words*

original key

THOMAS HARDY

BENJAMIN BRITTEN

© Copyright 1994 by Boosey & Hawkes Music Publishers Ltd.

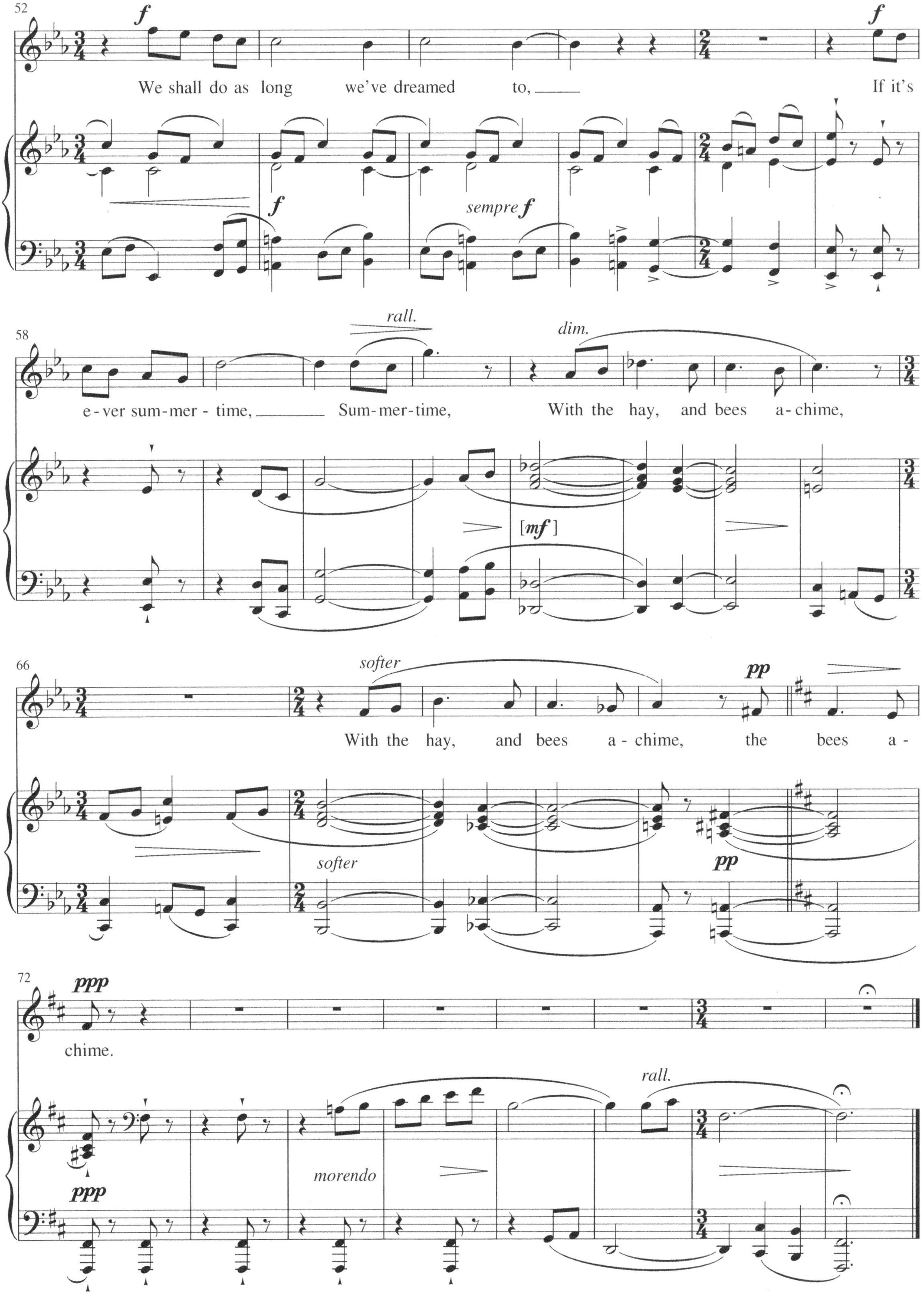
52
f
We shall do as long we've dreamed to,
If it's
f
sempre f
58
rall.
dim.
e-ver sum-mer-time, Sum-mer-time, With the hay, and bees a-chime,
[mf]
66
softer
pp
With the hay, and bees a-chime, the bees a-
softer
pp
72
ppp
chime.
rall.
morendo
ppp

At the mid hour of night
(*Molly, my Dear*)
original key

THOMAS MOORE
from *Irish Melodies*

Arranged by
BENJAMIN BRITTEN

© Copyright 1960 by Boosey & Co. Ltd.
All rights reserved

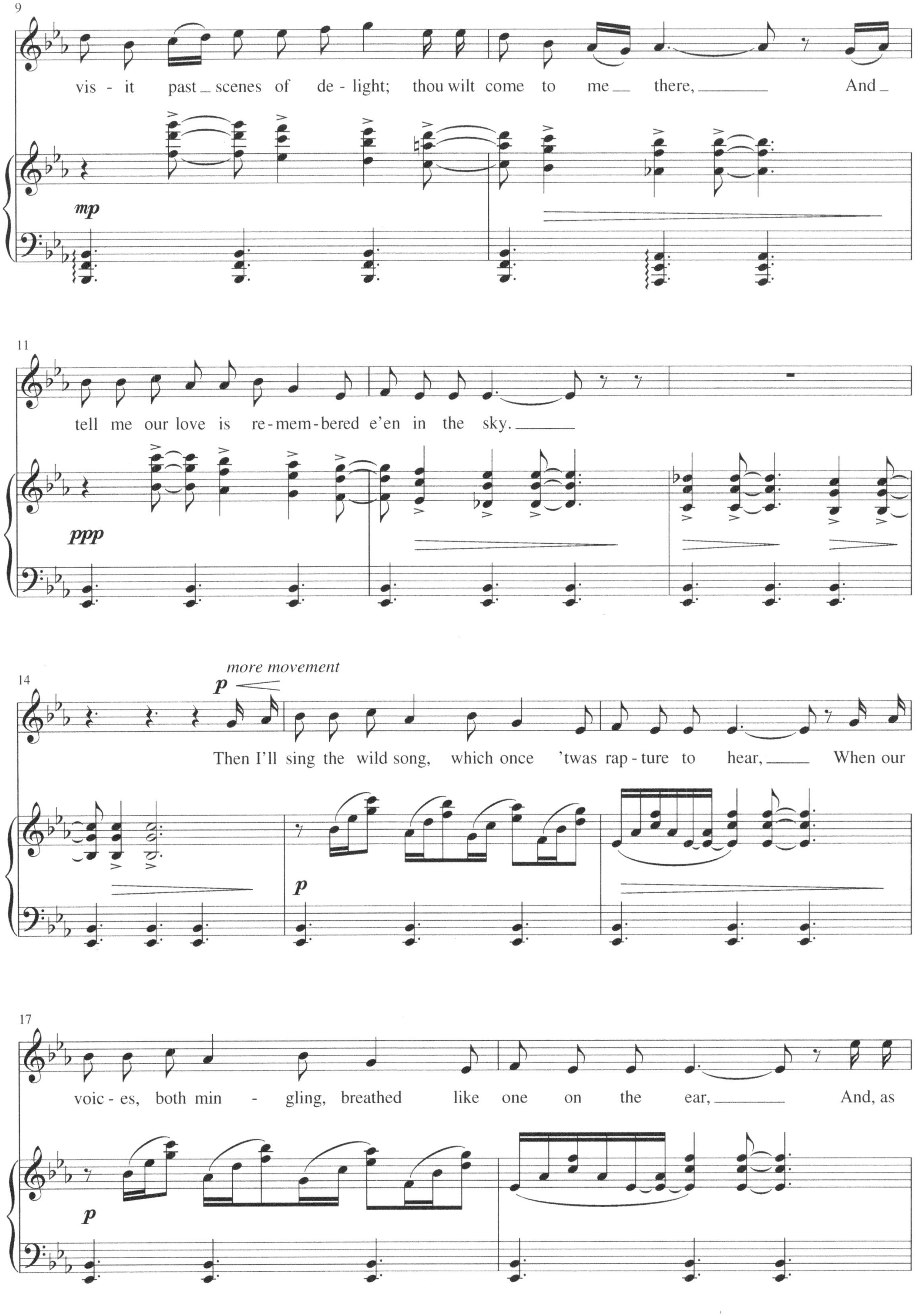
9
vis - it past scenes of de - light; thou wilt come to me there, And
mp
11
tell me our love is re-mem-bered e'en in the sky.
ppp
14
more movement
p
Then I'll sing the wild song, which once 'twas rap - ture to hear, When our
p
17
voic - es, both min - gling, breathed like one on the ear, And, as
p

66

To Clytie Mundy

The Salley Gardens

Irish Tune

original key

* W.B. YEATS

Arranged by
BENJAMIN BRITTEN

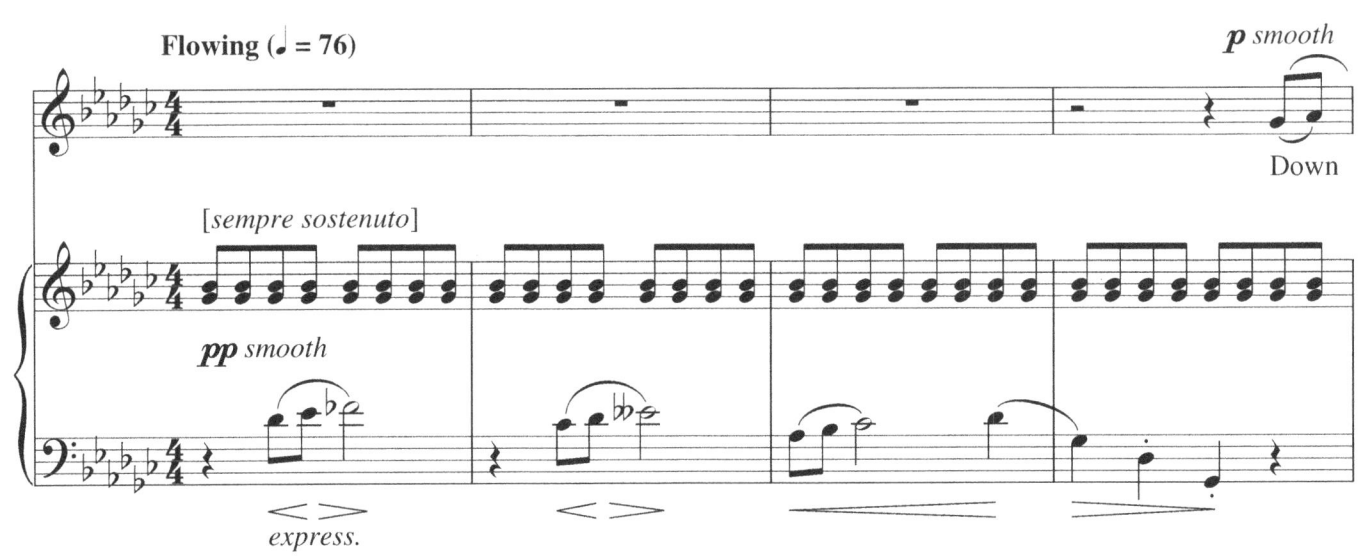

*The words of this song are reprinted from "Collected Poems of W. B. Yeats" by permission of Mrs. Yeats.

© Copyright 1943 in U.S.A. by Boosey & Co. Ltd.
Copyright for all countries
All rights reserved

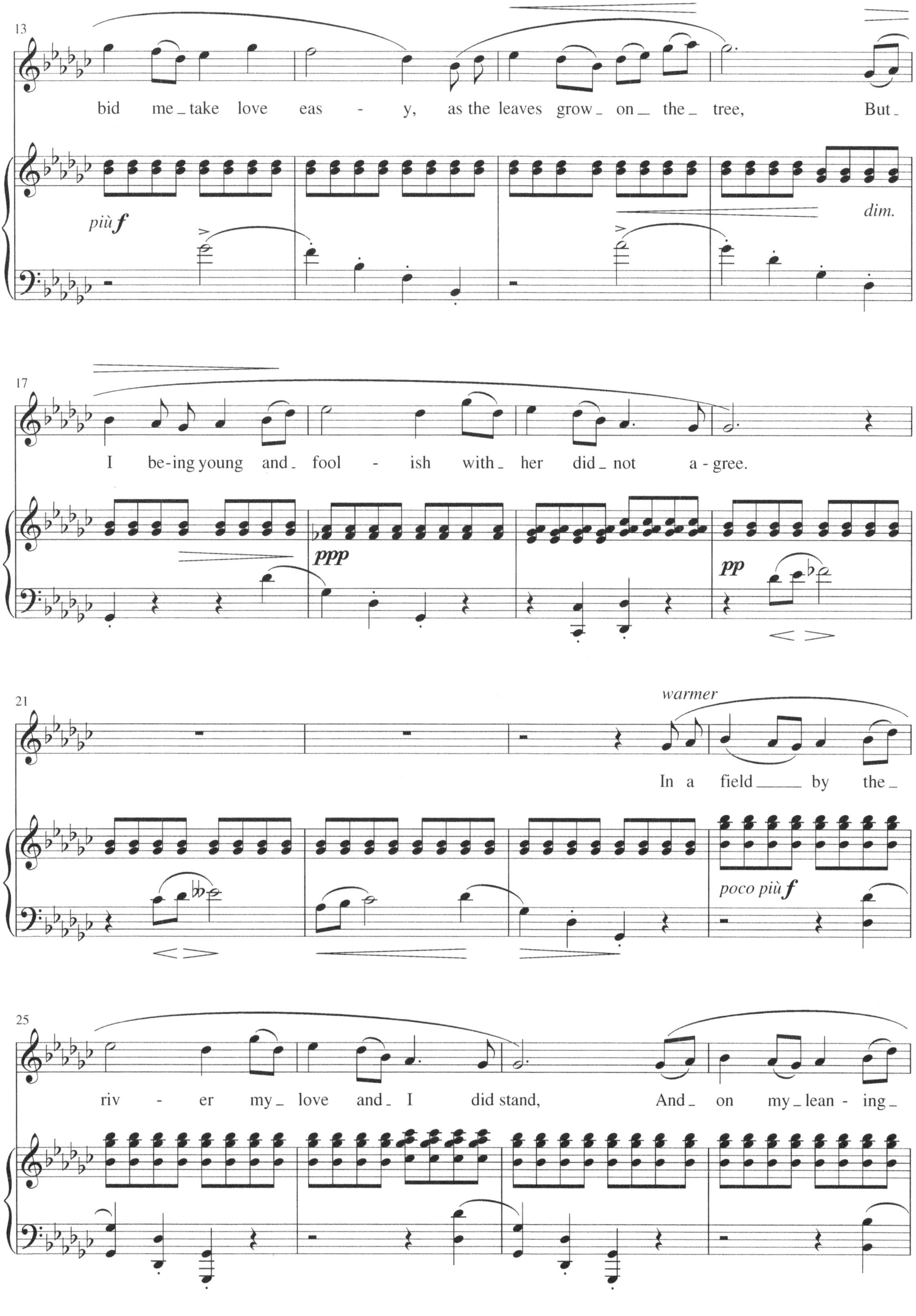
13
bid me _ take love eas - y, as the leaves grow _ on _ the _ tree, But _
più f
dim.
17
I be-ing young and _ fool - ish with _ her did _ not a - gree.
ppp
pp
21
warmer
In a field ___ by the _
poco più f
25
riv - er my _ love and _ I did stand, And _ on my _ lean - ing _

These, My Ophelia

original key

ARCHIBALD MACLEISH THEODORE CHANLER

Copyright 1936 by Cos Cob Press Inc., New York, Renewed 1962.
Copyright and renewal assigned to Boosey & Hawkes, Inc.
Copyright for all countries. All rights reserved.

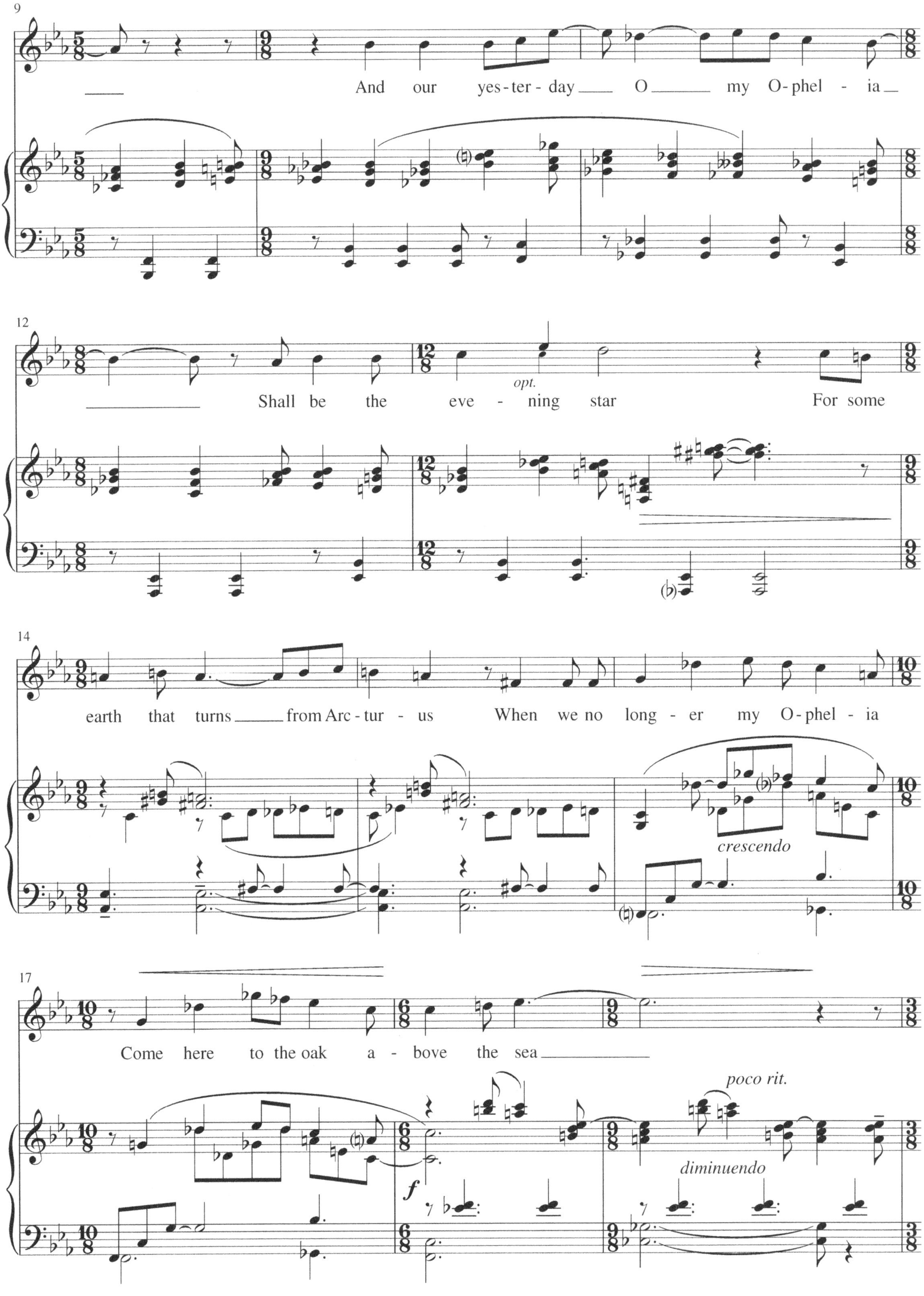
9
And our yes-ter-day O my O-phel - ia
12
Shall be the eve - ning star For some
opt.
14
earth that turns from Arc-tur - us When we no long - er my O-phel - ia
crescendo
17
Come here to the oak a - bove the sea
f
poco rit.
diminuendo

The Seal Man

"Them that live in the water, they have ways of calling people."
original key: a major 2nd lower

JOHN MASEFIELD
from *A Mainsail Haul*

REBECCA CLARKE

Copyright © 1926 by Hawkes & Son (London) Ltd. Copyright Renewed.
New transposition © 2006 by Boosey & Hawkes Music Publishers Ltd.
Words used by permission.

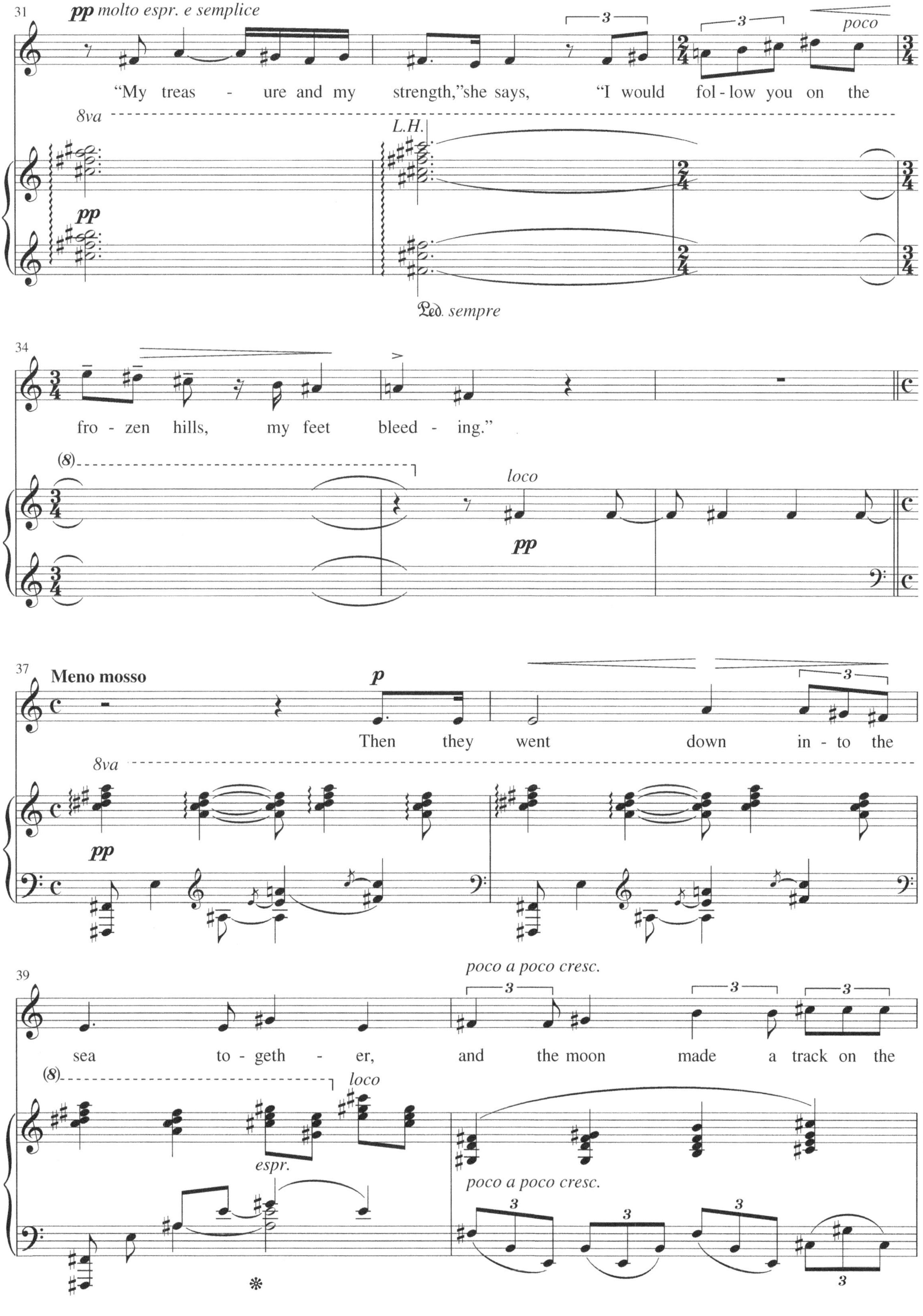
31
pp molto espr. e semplice
"My treas - ure and my strength," she says, "I would fol - low you on the
poco
8va
L.H.
pp
Ped. sempre
34
fro - zen hills, my feet bleed - ing."
(8)
loco
pp
37
Meno mosso
p
Then they went down in - to the
8va
pp
39
poco a poco cresc.
sea to - geth - er, and the moon made a track on the
(8)
loco
espr.
poco a poco cresc.

Down by the salley gardens

original key: E minor

W.B. YEATS

REBECCA CLARKE

© Copyright 1924 by Winthrop Rogers Ltd.
New transposition © 2006 by Boosey & Hawkes Music Publishers Ltd.
Words used by kind permission

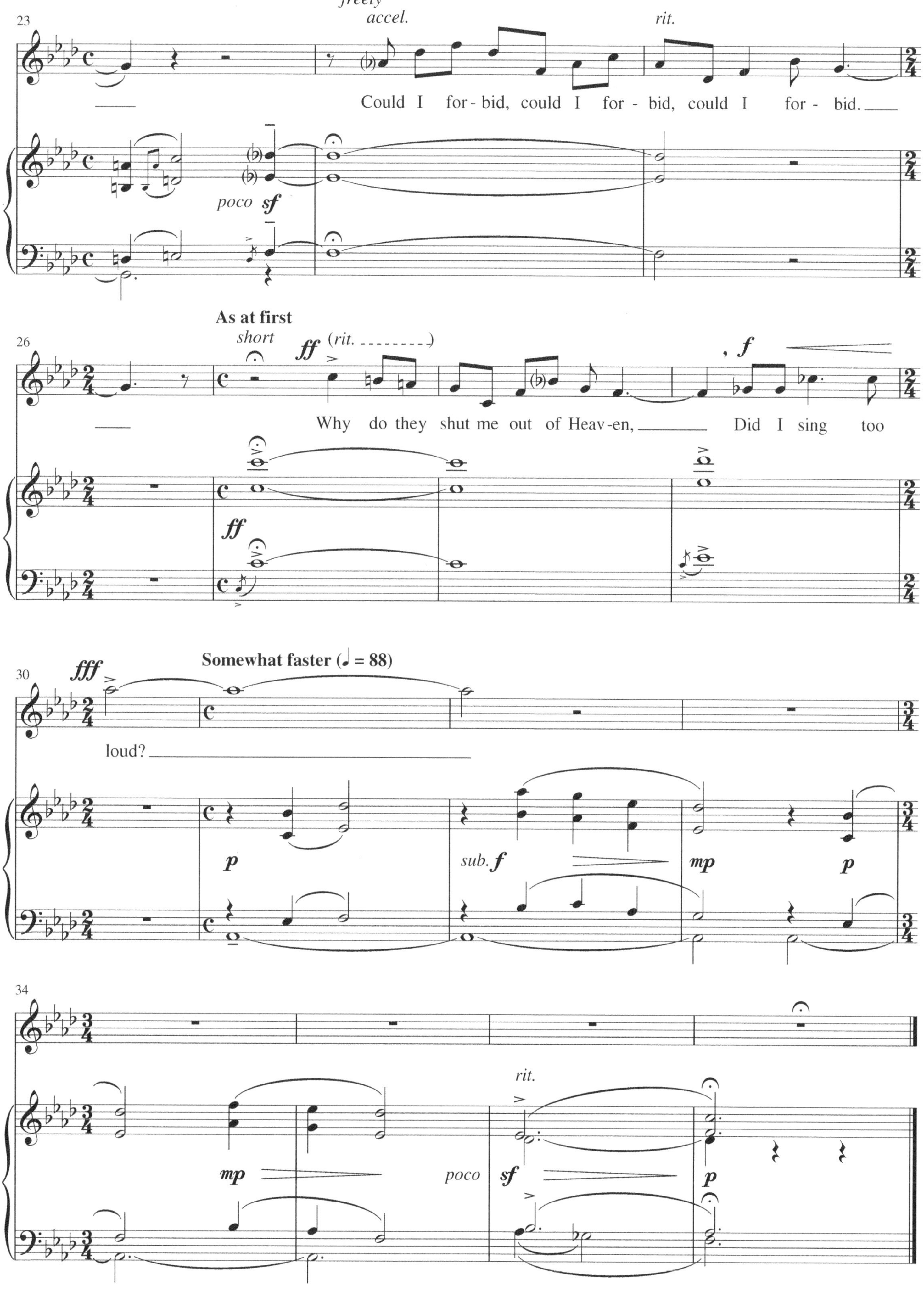

freely
accel.
rit.
Could I for-bid, could I for-bid, could I for-bid.
poco sf
As at first
short
ff (rit.)
Why do they shut me out of Heav-en,
f
Did I sing too
fff
Somewhat faster (♩ = 88)
loud?
p
sub. f
mp
p
mp
poco sf
rit.
p

Heart, we will forget him

To Marcelle de Manziarly

from *Twelve Poems of Emily Dickinson*
original key

EMILY DICKINSON AARON COPLAND

Lyrics:
Heart, we will forget him, You and I, to-night.
You may forget the warmth he gave. I will forget the light.

* Grace note on the beat

© Copyright 1951 by The Aaron Copland Fund For Music, Inc. Copyright Renewed.
Boosey & Hawkes, Inc., Sole Publisher & Licensee.
Copyright for all countries. All rights reserved.
Text from *Poems of Emily Dickinson*, edited by Martha Dickinson
and Alfred Leete Hampson, by permission of Little, Brown and Company.

Poet's Song
original key

*e.e. cummings

AARON COPLAND

* Copyright 1926 by Boni & Liveright, poem used by permission of the publishers
Copyright 1935 by Cos Cob Press Inc., Renewed 1962
Copyright assigned to The Aaron Copland Fund for Music, Inc.
Boosey & Hawkes, Inc. Sole publisher & Licensee.

Königstein
Aug. 1927

At the River
(Hymn Tune)
from *Old American Songs, Set II*
original key: E♭ Major

ANONYMOUS
AARON COPLAND

© Copyright 1954 by The Aaron Copland Fund for Music, Inc. Copyright Renewed.
New transposition © 2005 by The Aaron Copland Fund for Music, Inc.
Boosey & Hawkes, Inc., Sole Publisher & Licensee.
All rights reserved.

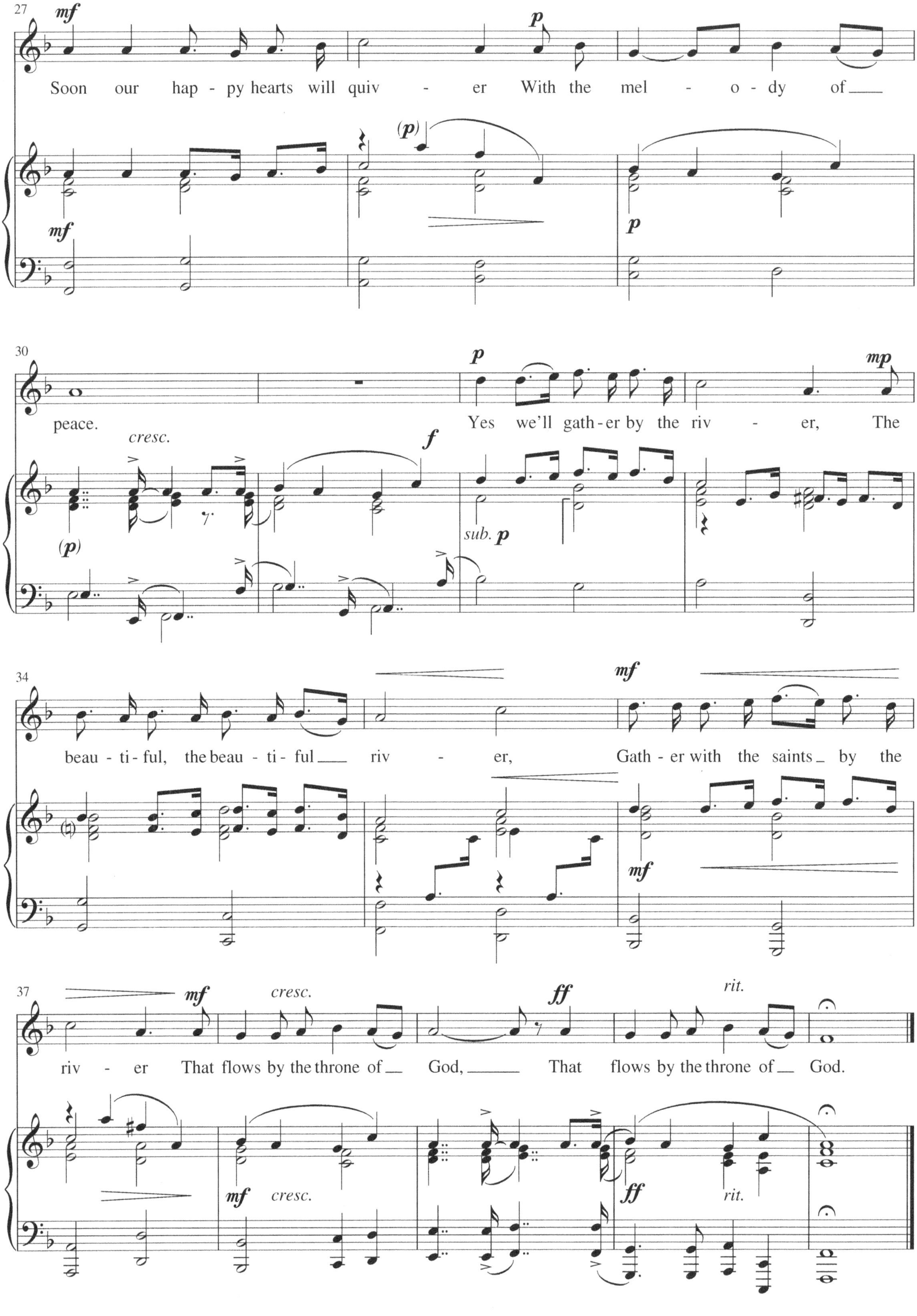
Soon our hap - py hearts will quiv - er With the mel - o - dy of
peace. Yes we'll gath - er by the riv - er, The
beau - ti - ful, the beau - ti - ful riv - er, Gath - er with the saints by the
riv - er That flows by the throne of God, That flows by the throne of God.
mf p (p) cresc. f sub. p mp mf ff rit.

The Little Horses

(Lullaby)

from *Old American Songs, Set II*

original key: E minor

ANONYMOUS

AARON COPLAND

© Copyright 1954 by The Aaron Copland Fund for Music, Inc. Copyright Renewed.
New transposition © 2005 by The Aaron Copland Fund for Music, Inc.
Boosey & Hawkes, Inc., Sole Publisher & Licensee.
All rights reserved.

Acrostic Song
(Alice Pleasance Liddell)

from *Final Alice*
original key

LEWIS CARROLL

DAVID DEL TREDICI

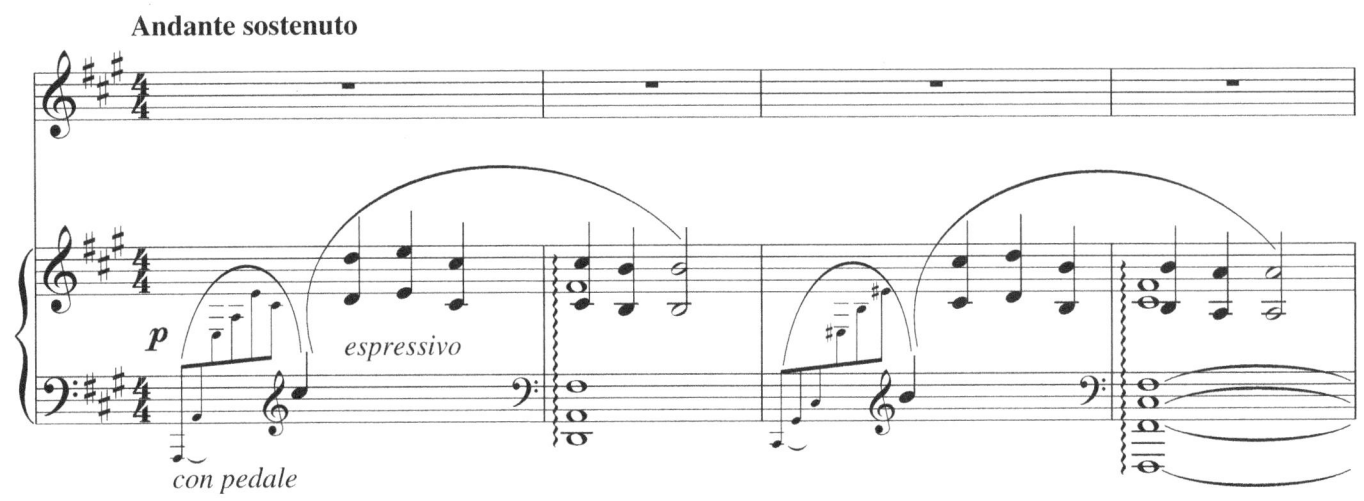

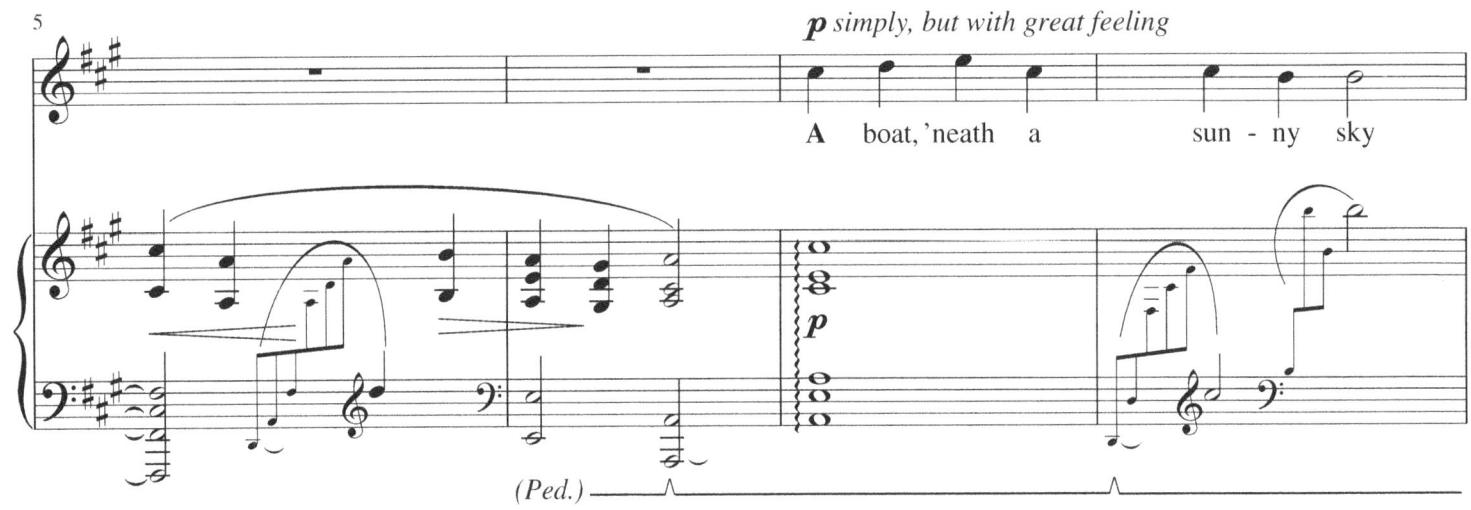

A boat, 'neath a sun-ny sky

Lin-g'ring on-ward dream-i-ly In an ev'-ning of Ju-ly—

© Copyright 1978 by Boosey & Hawkes, Inc.
This arrangement © 1984 by Boosey & Hawkes, Inc.
Copyright for all countries.   All rights reserved.

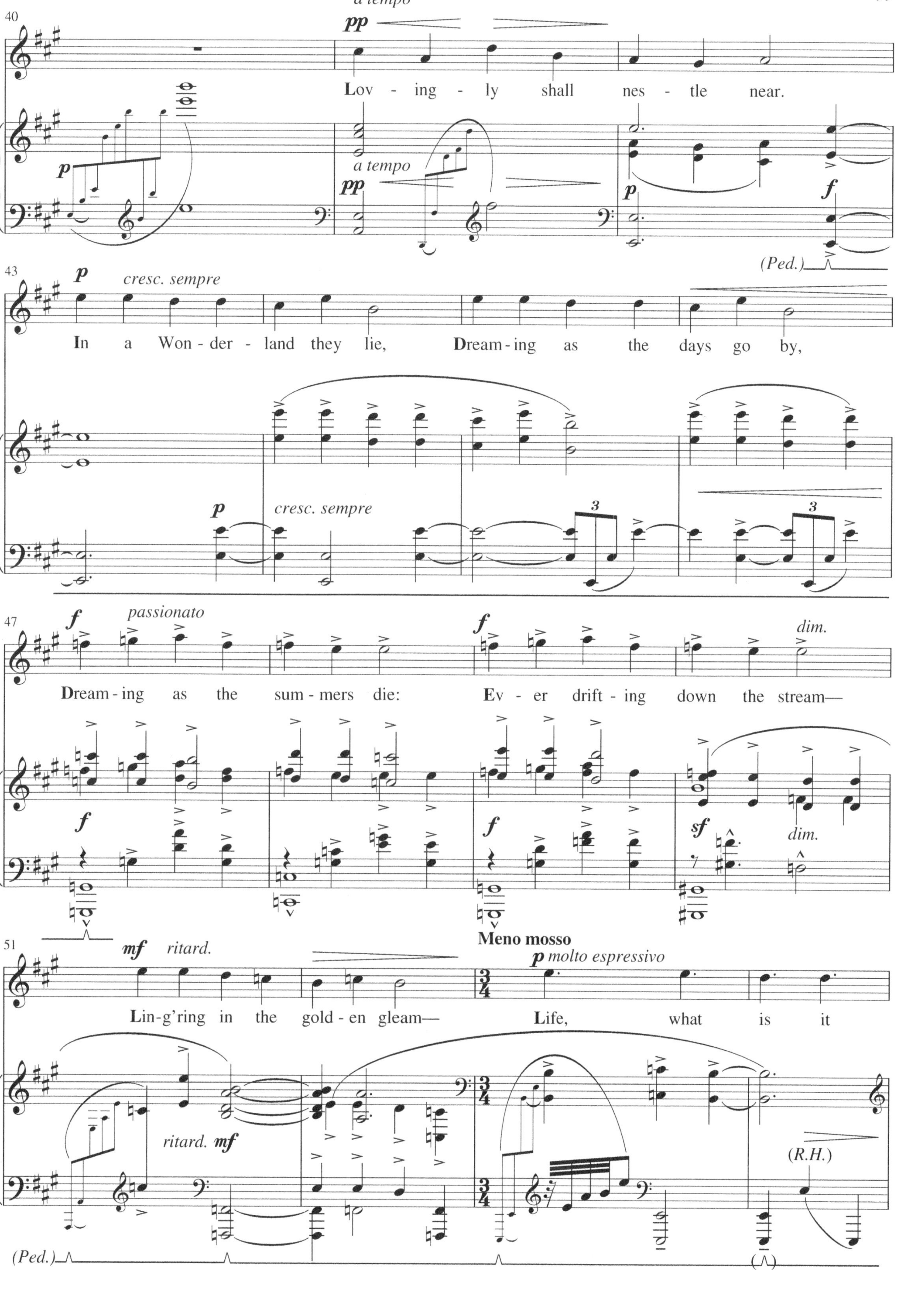
a tempo
pp
Lov - ing - ly shall nes - tle near.
p
a tempo
pp
p
f
(Ped.)
p cresc. sempre
In a Won - der - land they lie, Dream - ing as the days go by,
p
cresc. sempre
3
3
f passionato
Dream - ing as the sum - mers die:
f
Ev - er drift - ing down the stream—
dim.
f
f
sf
dim.
mf ritard.
Lin - g'ring in the gold - en gleam—
Meno mosso
p molto espressivo
Life, what is it
ritard. mf
(R.H.)
(Ped.)

Central Park at Dusk
original key

SARA TEASDALE*

JOHN DUKE

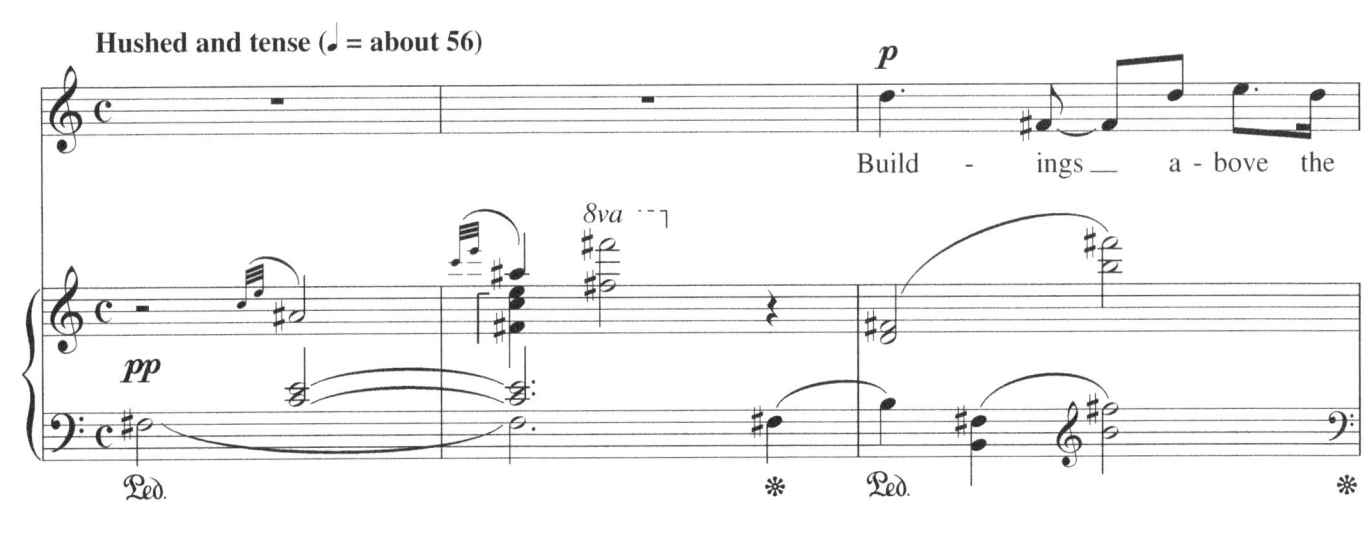

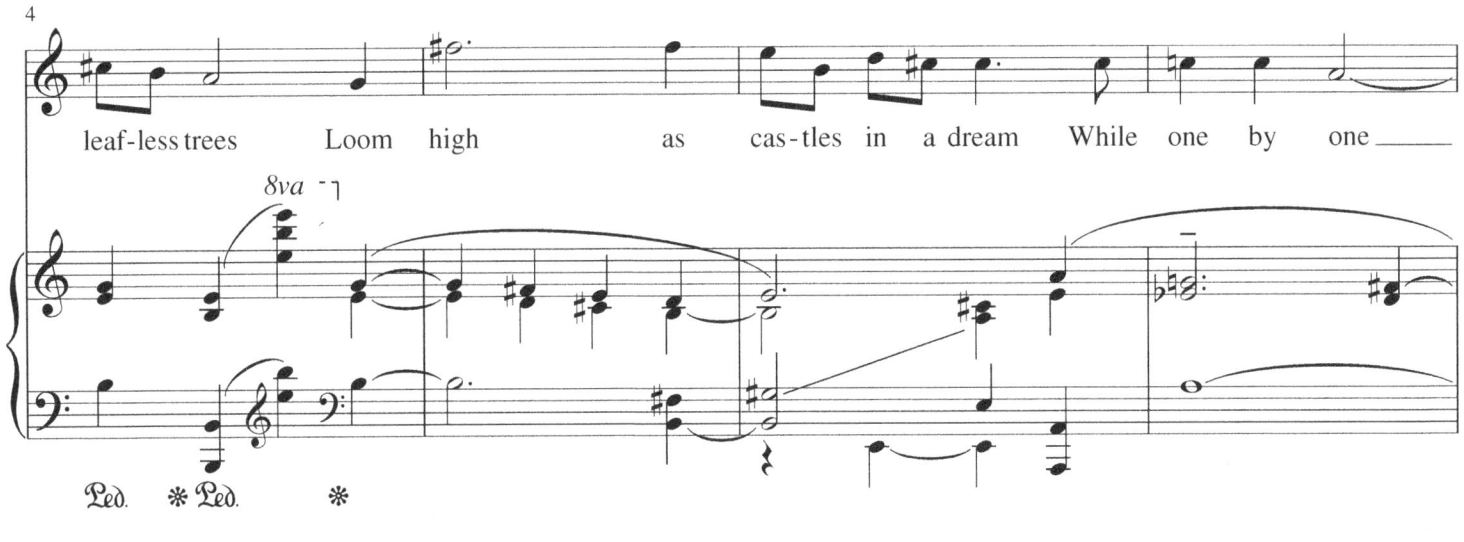

*From "Collected Poems" by Sara Teasdale (Macmillan)

© Copyright 1949 by Boosey & Hawkes, Inc. Copyright renewed.
Copyright for all countries. All rights reserved.

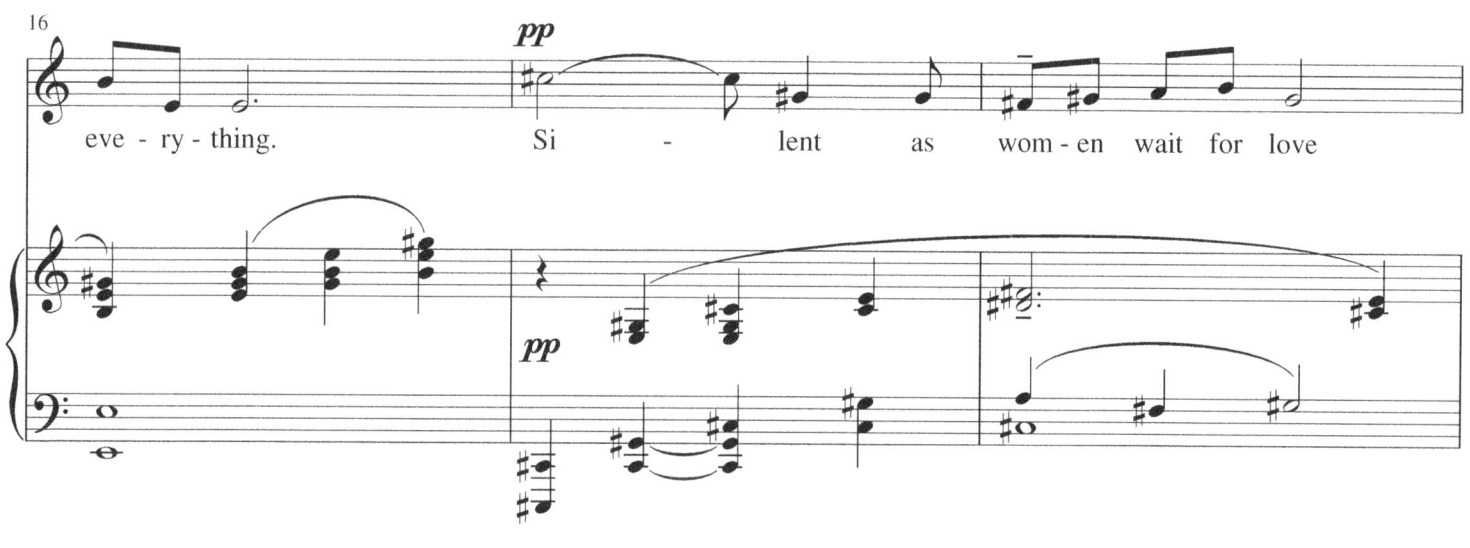

There will be stars
original key

SARA TEASDALE*

JOHN DUKE

*From "Collected Poems" by Sara Teasdale (Macmillan)

© Copyright 1953 by Boosey & Hawkes, Inc. Copyright renewed.
Copyright for all countries. All rights reserved.

Spring Sorrow

original key: F Major

RUPERT BROOKE

JOHN IRELAND

This Poem is reprinted from "1914 and other Poems" by Rupert Brooke,
by permission of the Literary Executor and Messrs Sidgwick and Jackson Ltd.

© Copyright 1918 by Winthrop Rogers Ltd.
New transposition © 2006 by Boosey & Hawkes Music Publishers Ltd.
All rights reserved
Sole Selling Agents Boosey & Hawkes Music Publishers Ltd.

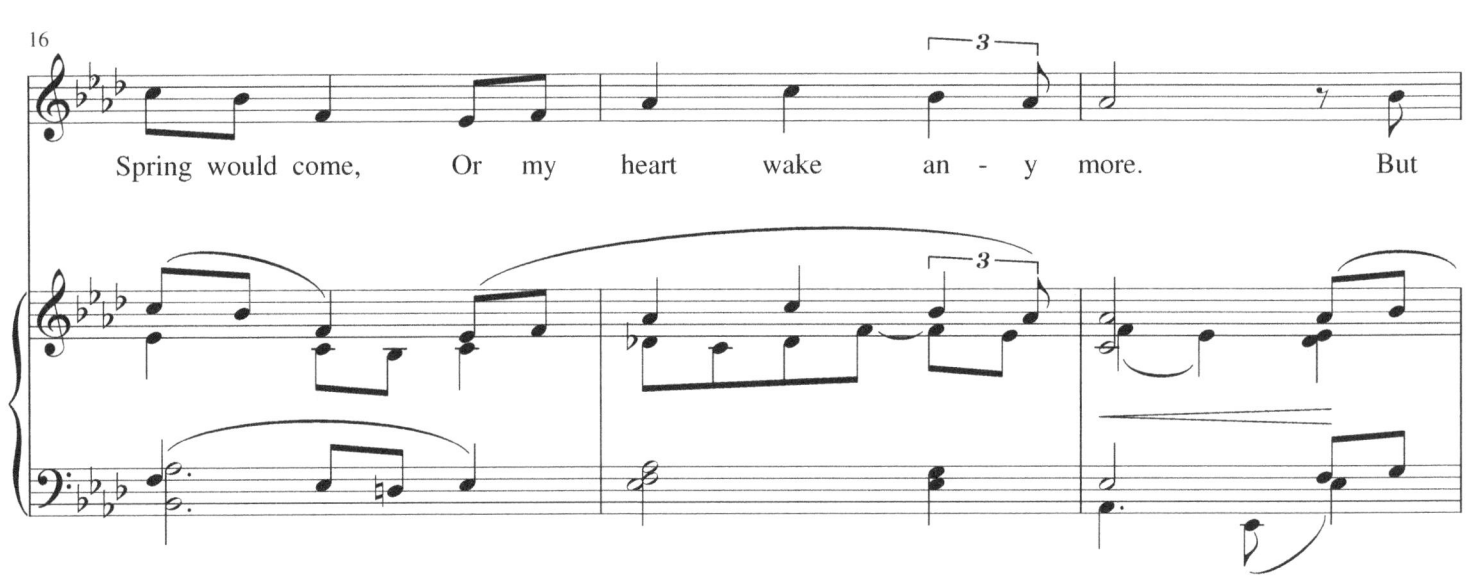

April, 1918

Fear no more the heat o' the sun

from *Let us garlands bring*

original key: B♭ Major

WILLIAM SHAKESPEARE

GERALD FINZI

© Copyright 1942 by Boosey & Co. Ltd. Copyright Renewed.
New transposition © 2006 by Boosey & Hawkes Music Publishers Ltd.
Copyright for all countries

It was a lover and his lass

from *Let us garlands bring*

original key: E Major

WILLIAM SHAKESPEARE*

GERALD FINZI

*The 1623 Folio text is here collated with the version in Thomas Morley's "The First book of Ayres" 1600.

© Copyright 1942 by Boosey & Co. Ltd. Copyright Renewed.
New transposition © 2006 by Boosey & Hawkes Music Publishers Ltd.
Copyright for all countries

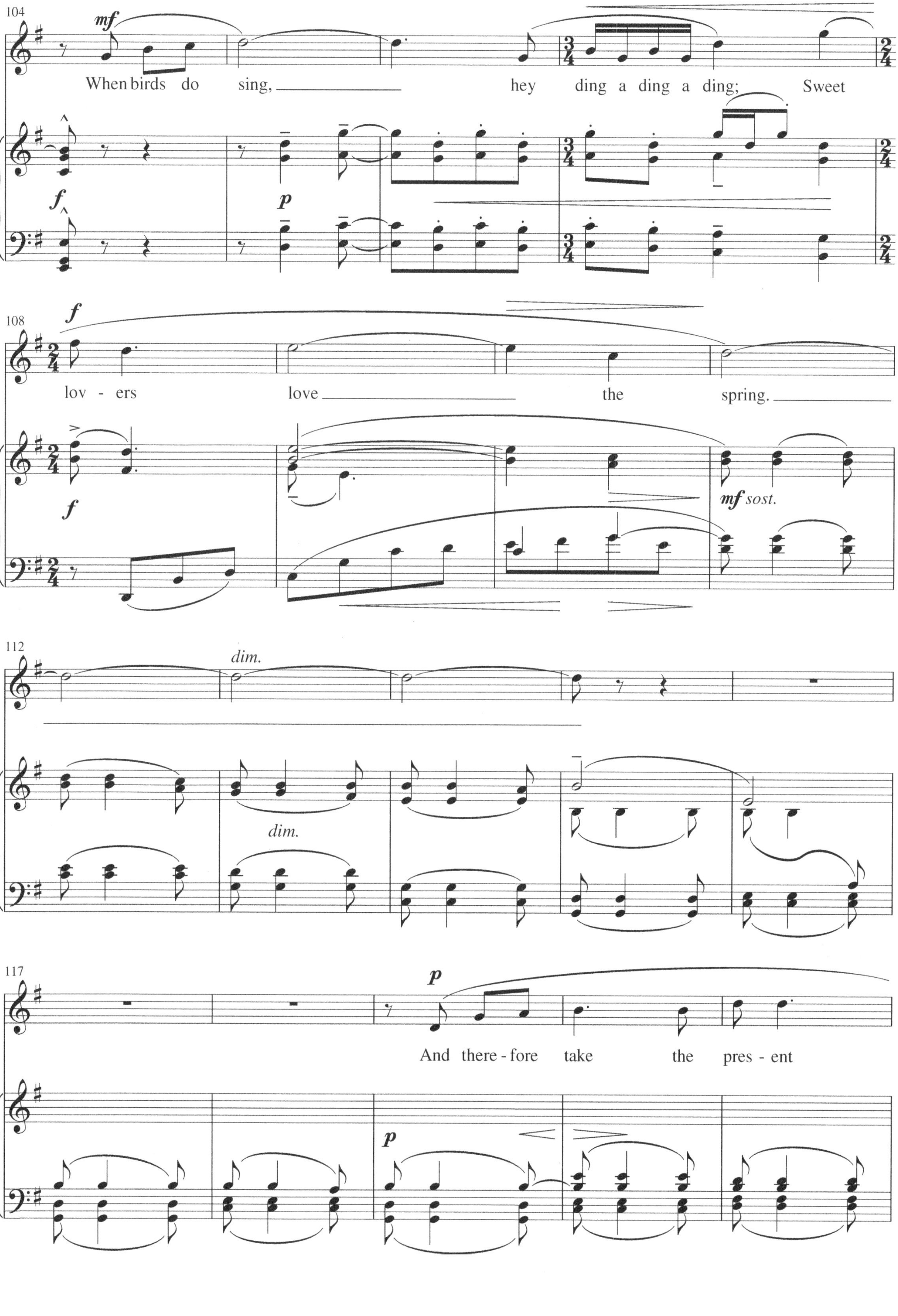
104
mf
When birds do sing, hey ding a ding a ding; Sweet
f
p
108
f
lov - ers love the spring.
f
mf sost.
112
dim.
dim.
117
p
And there - fore take the pres - ent
p

Oh fair to see

from *Oh Fair to See*
original key

CHRISTINA ROSSETTI

GERALD FINZI

© 1966 by Boosey & Co. Ltd. Copyright Renewed.
All rights reserved

Rain

from *Two Stevenson Songs*

original key for Unison Chorus: a minor 3rd lower

ROBERT LOUIS STEVENSON

CARLISLE FLOYD

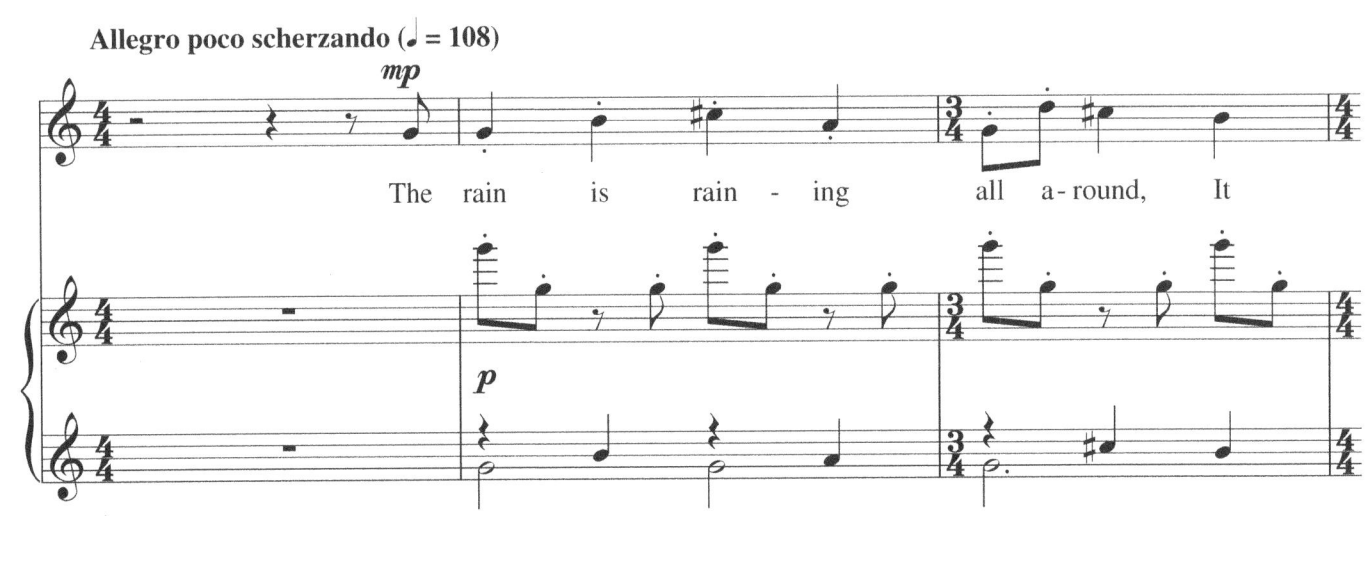

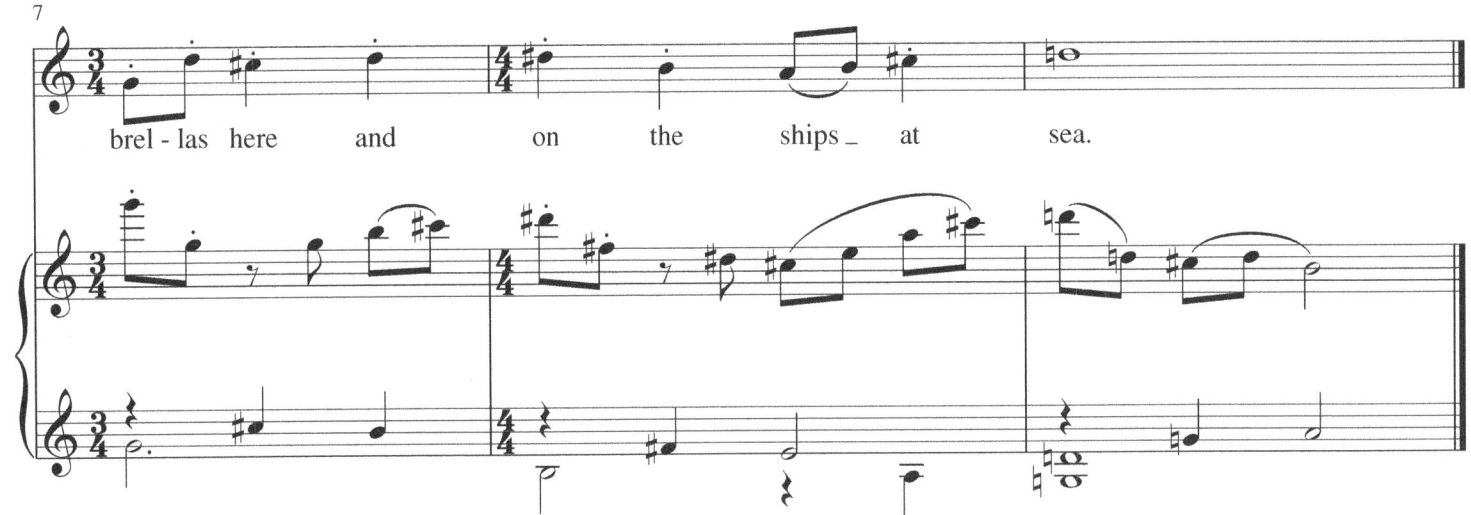

© Copyright 1967 by Boosey & Hawkes, Inc. Copyright Renewed.
New transposition © 2006 by Boosey & Hawkes, Inc.
Copyright for all countries. All rights reserved.

Where Go the Boats?

from *Two Stevenson Songs*
original key for Unison Chorus: C Major

ROBERT LOUIS STEVENSON
CARLISLE FLOYD

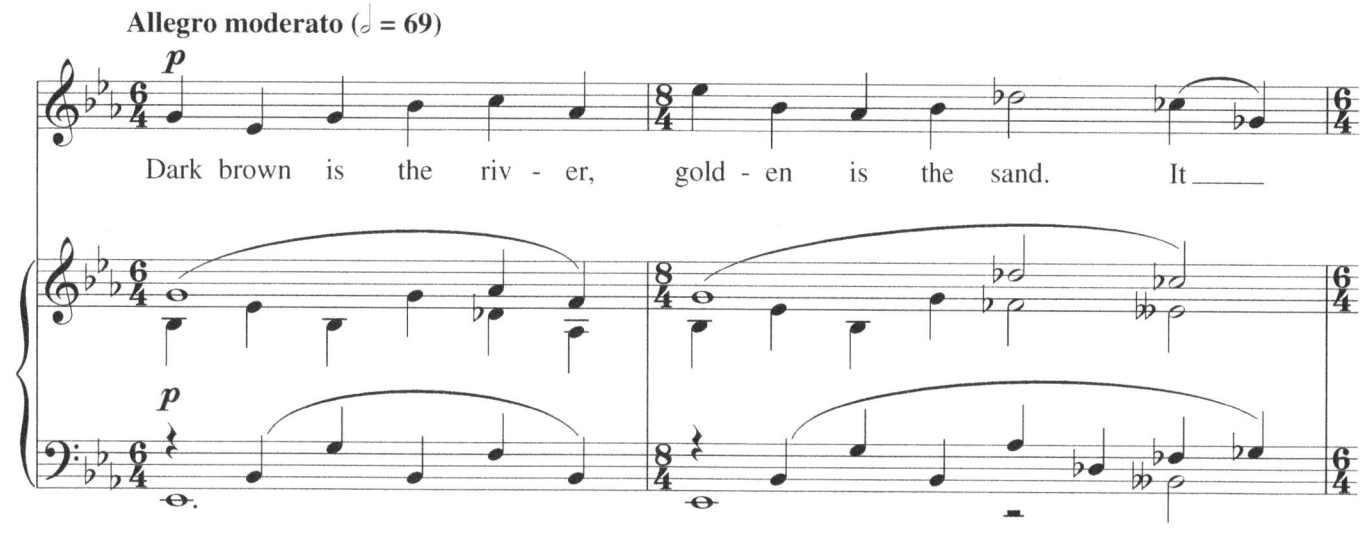

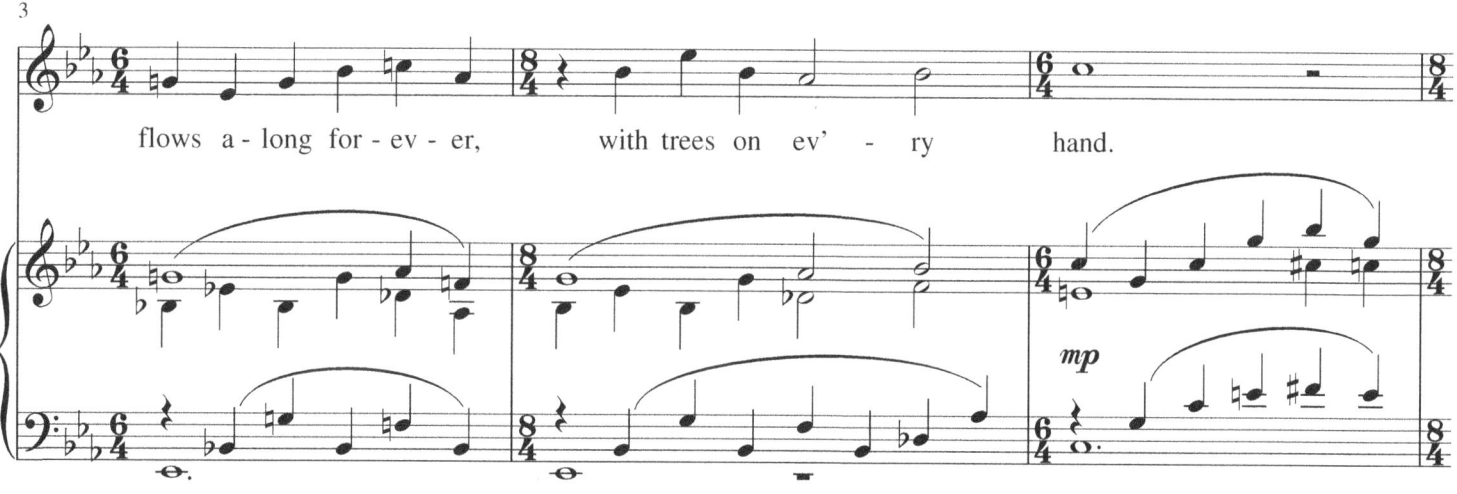

© Copyright 1967 by Boosey & Hawkes, Inc. Copyright Renewed.
New transposition © 2006 by Boosey & Hawkes, Inc.
Copyright for all countries. All rights reserved.

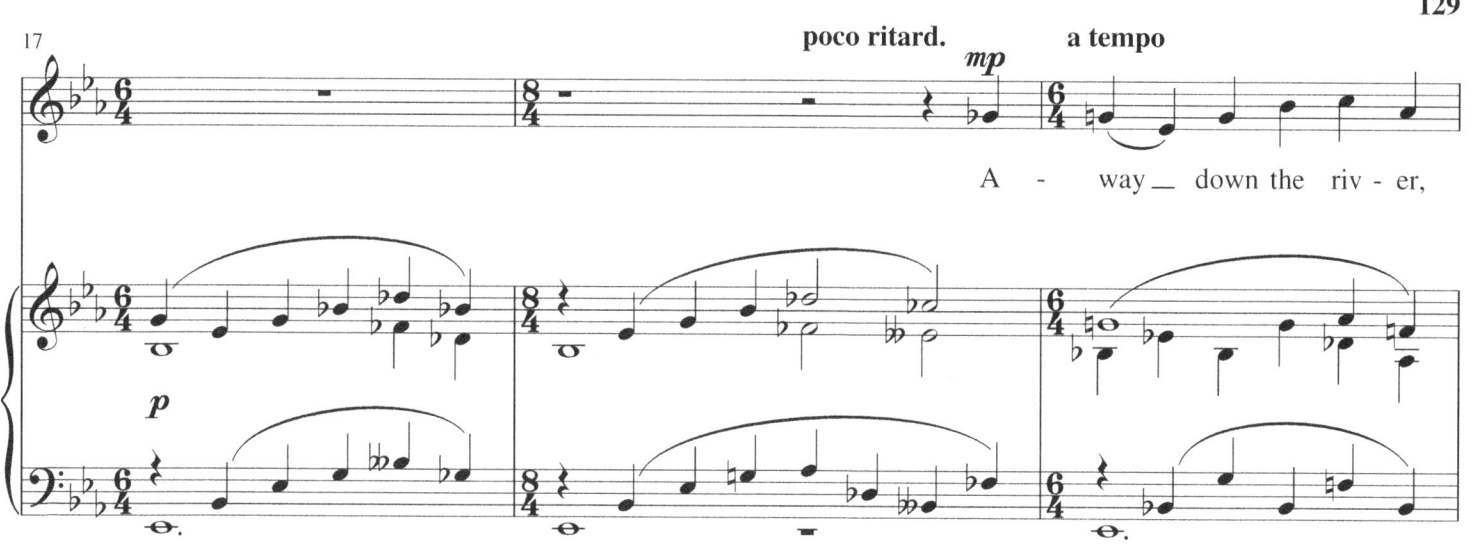
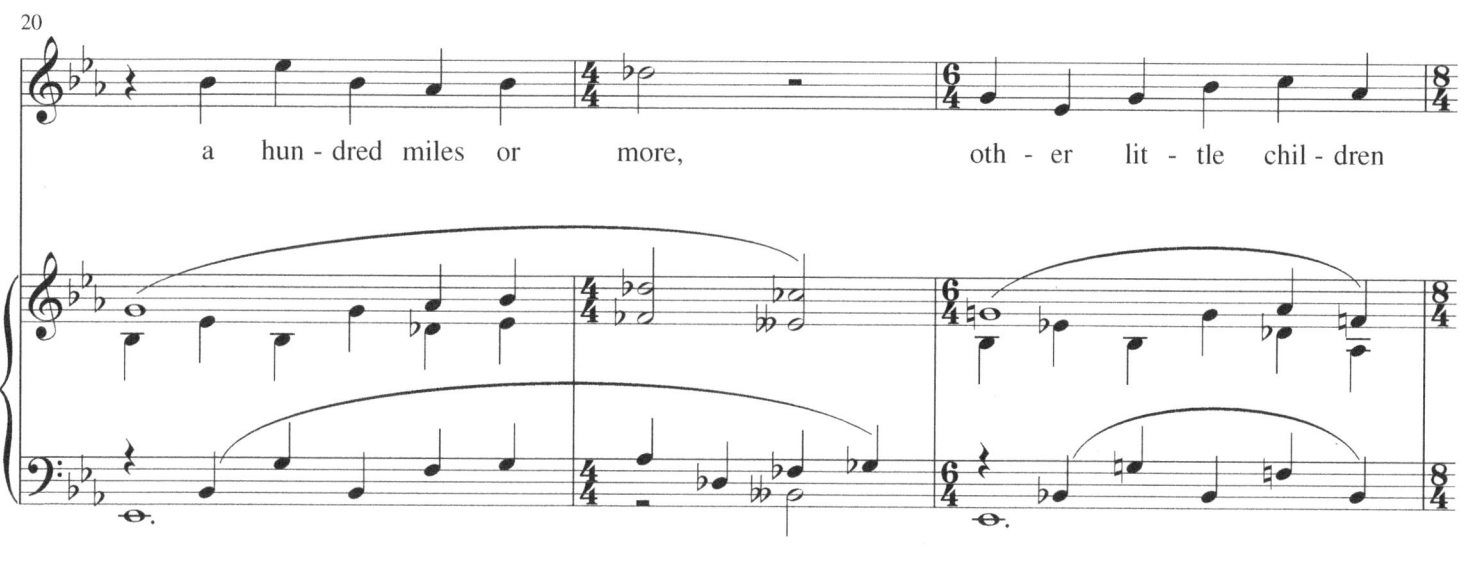

Sleep

To Emmy Hunt

from *Five Elizabethan Songs*

original key: B♭ minor

JOHN FLETCHER

IVOR GURNEY

© Copyright 1920 by Winthrop Rogers Ltd.

134

To Hester Berry

Money, O!

original key: G minor

W.H. DAVIES

MICHAEL HEAD

© Copyright 1929 by Boosey & Co. Ltd. Copyright Renewed.
New transposition © 2006 by Boosey & Hawkes Music Publishers Ltd.
All rights reserved
Sole Selling Agent Boosey & Hawkes Music Publishers Ltd.
Text used by permission of J. Cape Ltd.

Headley Down, Sept. 1928

138

To the memory of my grandmother

The Astronomers
(An Epitaph)
original key

Based on an inscription
found in Allegheny, Pa.

RICHARD HUNDLEY

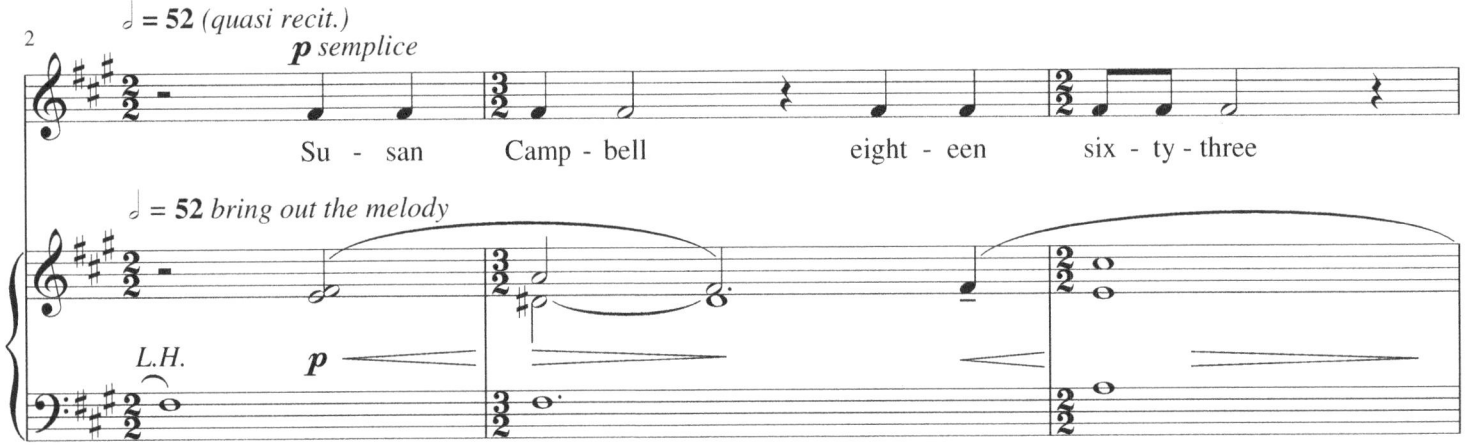

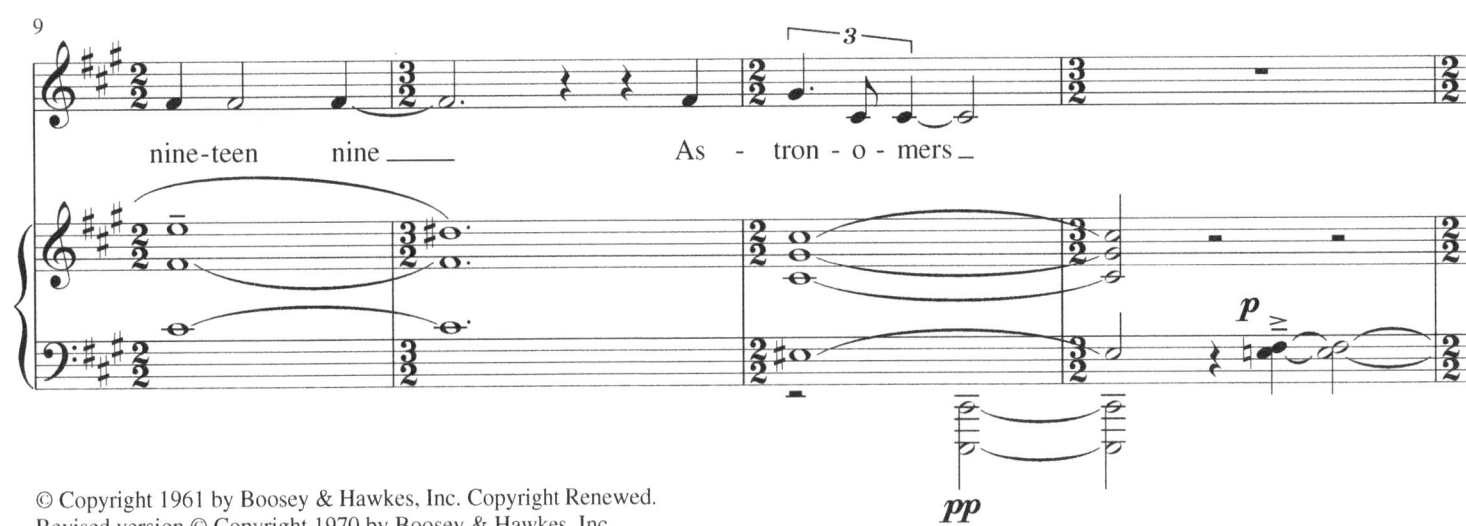

© Copyright 1961 by Boosey & Hawkes, Inc. Copyright Renewed.
Revised version © Copyright 1970 by Boosey & Hawkes, Inc.
Copyright for all countries. All rights reserved.

140

to Paul Sperry
Sweet Suffolk Owl
original key

Anonymous Verses 1619

RICHARD HUNDLEY

© Copyright 1981 by Boosey & Hawkes, Inc.
Copyright for all countries. All rights reserved.

June 5, 1979, New York City

142

to Paul Sperry
Waterbird
original key: A♭ Major

JAMES PURDY

RICHARD HUNDLEY

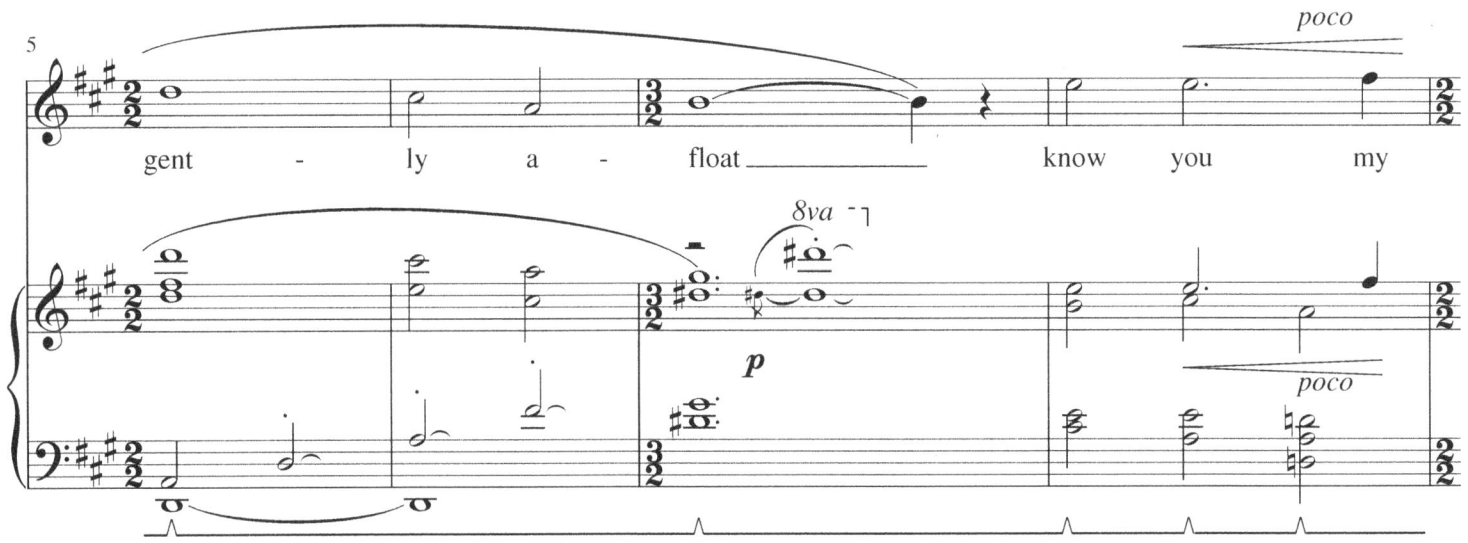

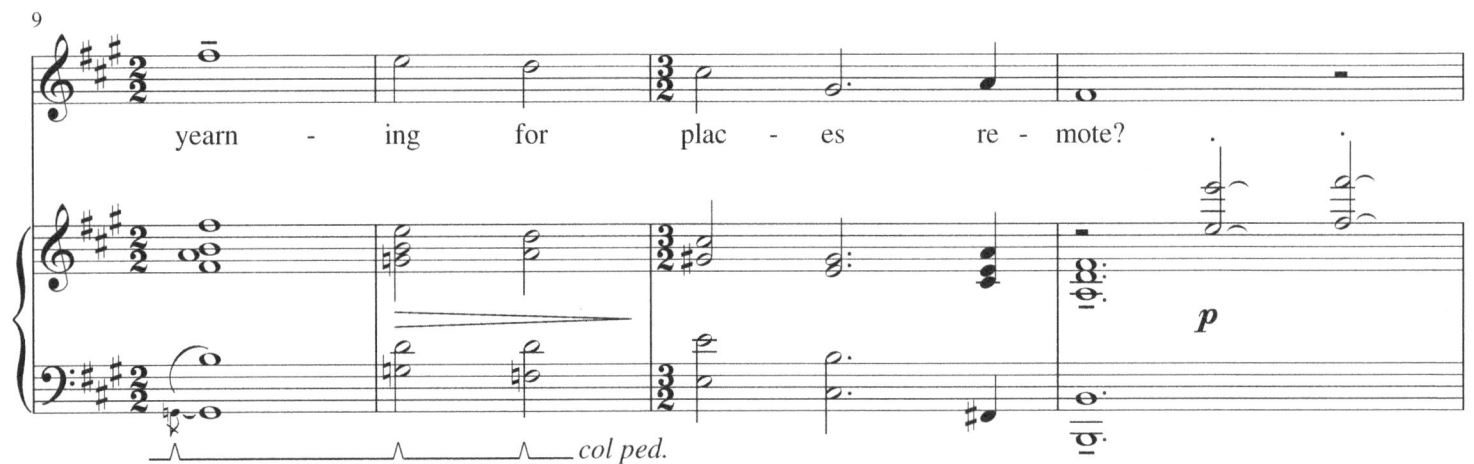

Text: Waterbird by James Purdy.
© Copyright by James Purdy. Used by permission.
© Copyright 1988 by Boosey & Hawkes, Inc.
New transposition © 2006 by Boosey & Hawkes, Inc.

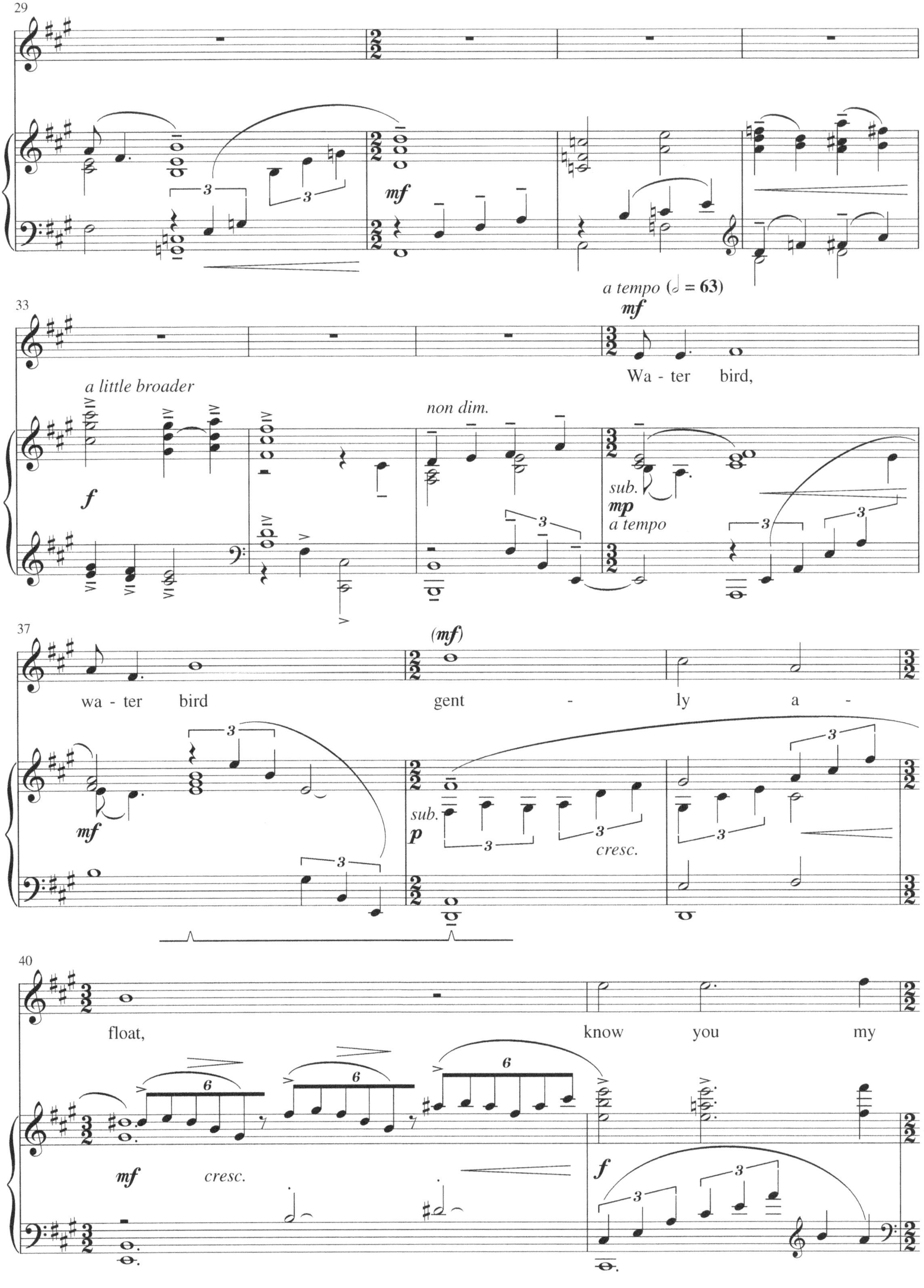
29
a tempo (𝅗𝅥 = 63)
mf
33
a little broader
f
non dim.
Wa - ter bird,
sub.
mp
a tempo
37
(mf)
wa - ter bird gent - ly a -
mf
sub.
p
cresc.
40
float, know you my
mf
cresc.
f

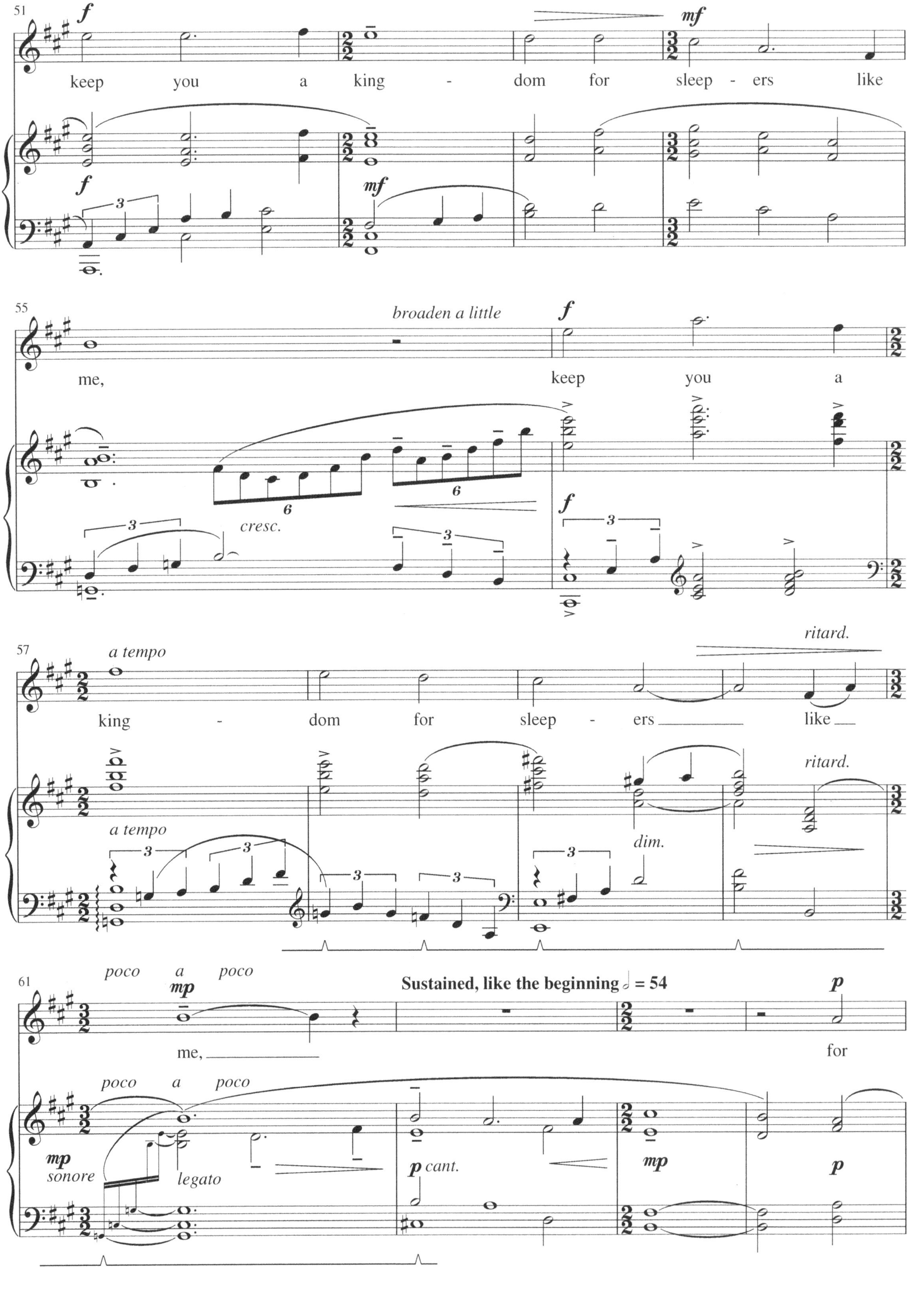
keep you a king - dom for sleep - ers like
me,
broaden a little
keep you a
a tempo
king - dom for sleep - ers like
ritard.
cresc.
dim.
poco a poco
me,
Sustained, like the beginning 𝅗𝅥 = 54
for
sonore
legato
p cant.

To Eva Raphael

How should I your true love know?

original key: G minor

WILLIAM SHAKESPEARE

ROGER QUILTER

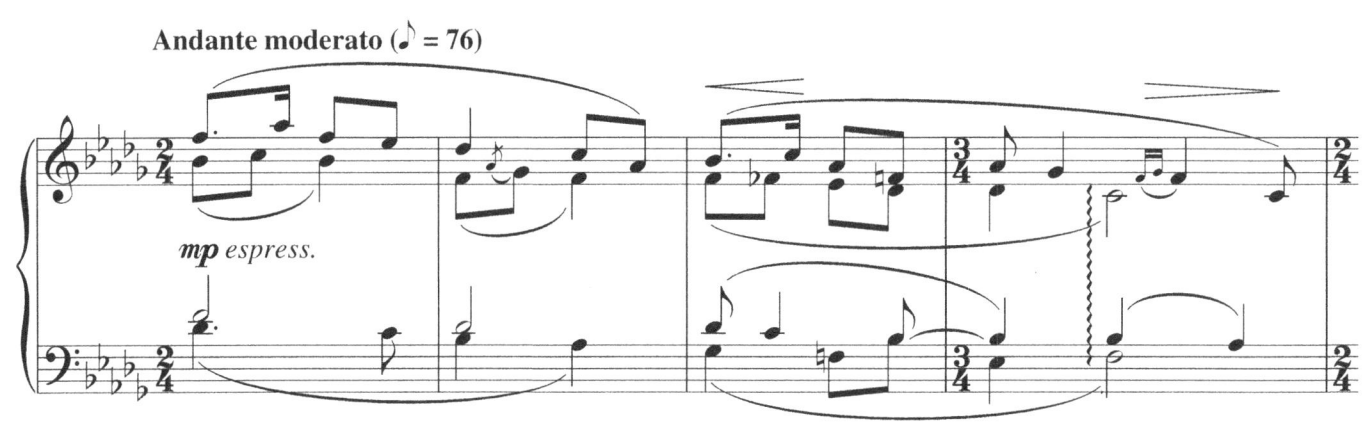

Copyright 1933 by Boosey & Co. Ltd. Copyright Renewed.
New transposition © 2006 by Boosey & Hawkes Music Publishers Ltd.

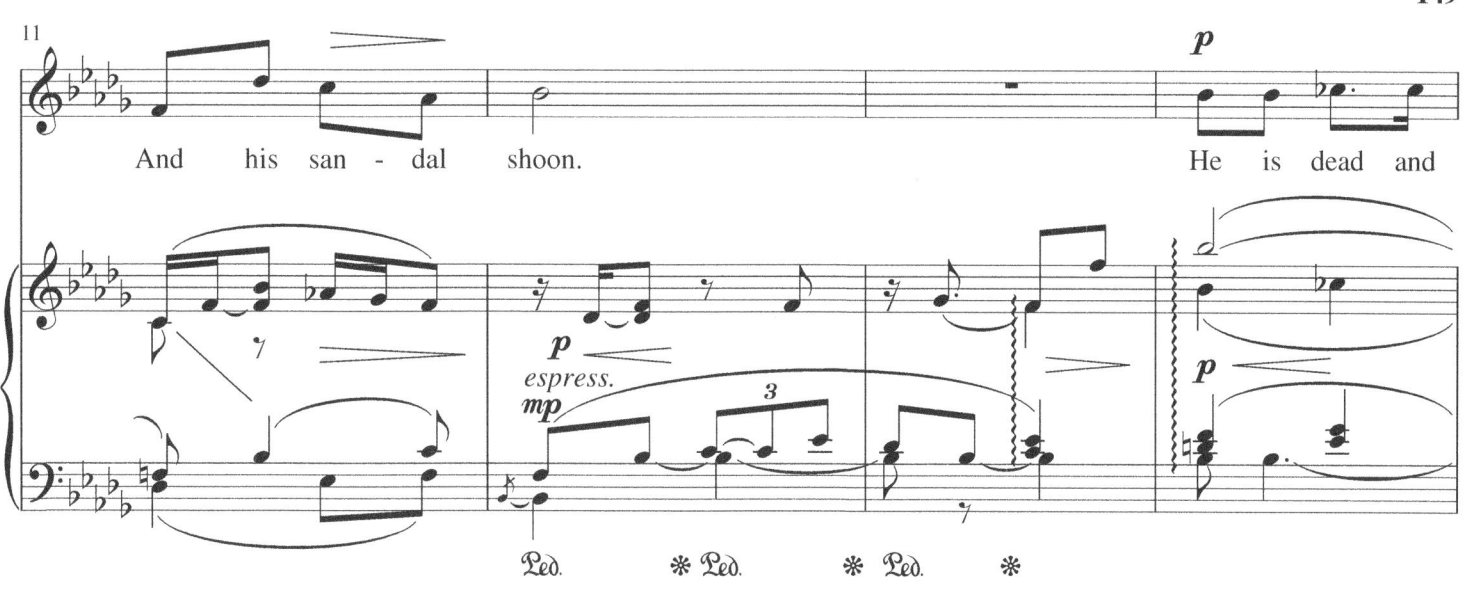

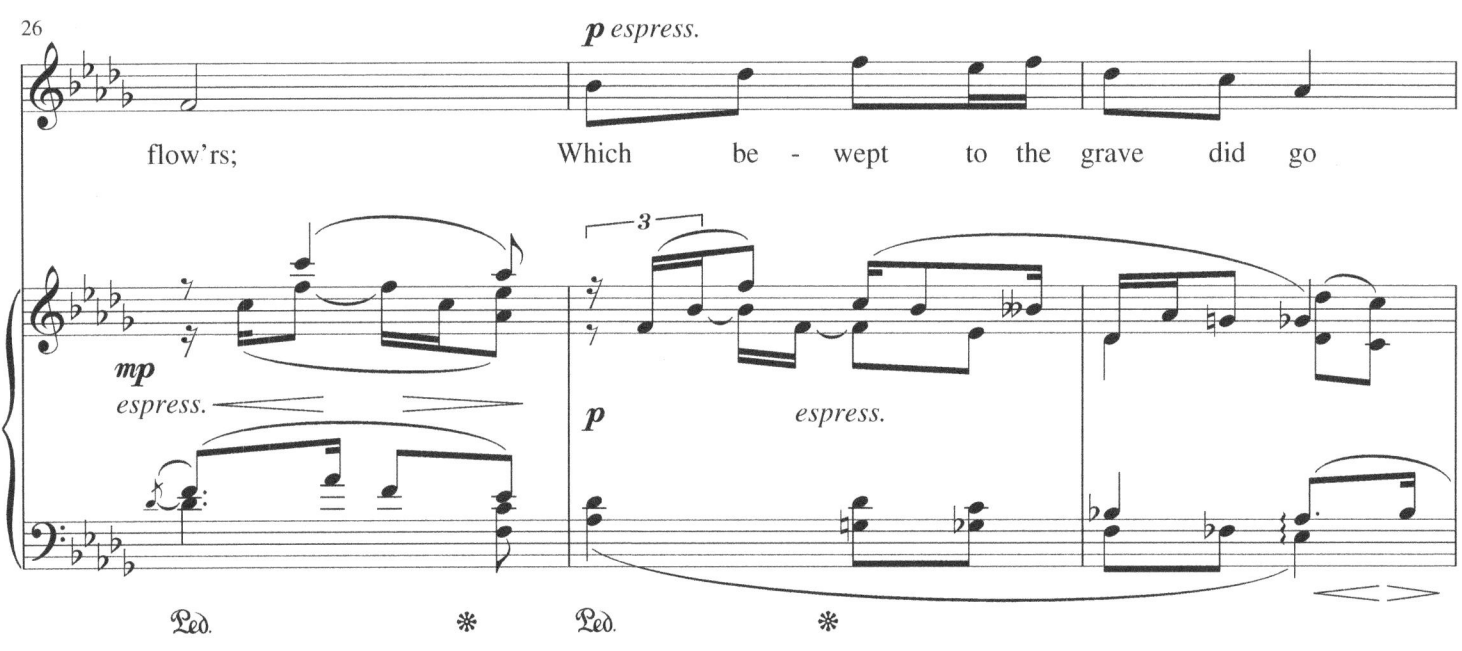
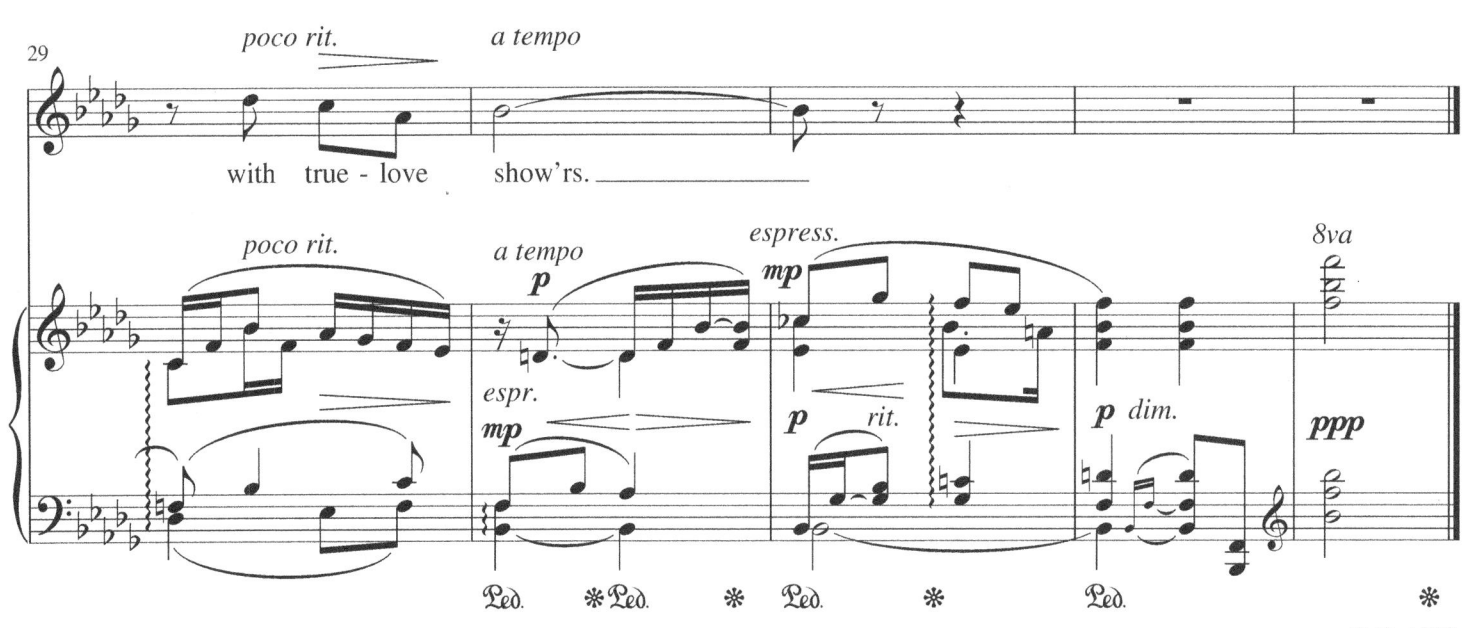

151

To the memory of my friend, Mrs. Cary-Elwes

Weep you no more
from *Seven Elizabethan Lyrics*
original key

ANONYMOUS ROGER QUILTER

Copyright © 1908 by Boosey & Co. Ltd. Copyright Renewed.

To the memory of my friend, Mrs. Cary-Elwes

My Life's Delight

from *Seven Elizabethan Lyrics*

original key

THOMAS CAMPION   ROGER QUILTER

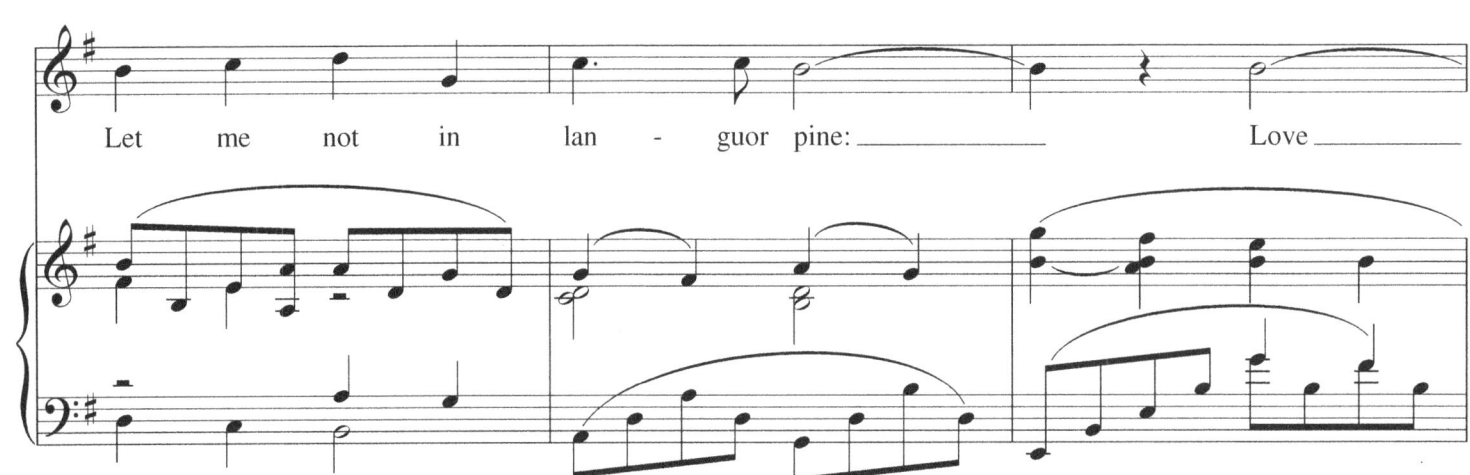

© Copyright 1908 by Boosey & Co. Ltd. Copyright Renewed.

158

to Jennie Tourel
Alleluia
original key

NED ROREM

© Copyright 1949 by Hargail Music, Inc.
© Copyright Renewed 1977 by Ned Rorem.
Copyright and Renewal assigned to Boosey & Hawkes, Inc.
Copyright for all countries. All rights reserved.

162

Ferry me across the water

from *The Nantucket Songs*
original key

CHRISTINA ROSSETTI

NED ROREM

© Copyright 1981 by Boosey & Hawkes, Inc.
Copyright for all countries. All rights reserved.

Jeanie with the Light Brown Hair

original key: D♭ Major

STEPHEN FOSTER
arranged by
NED ROREM

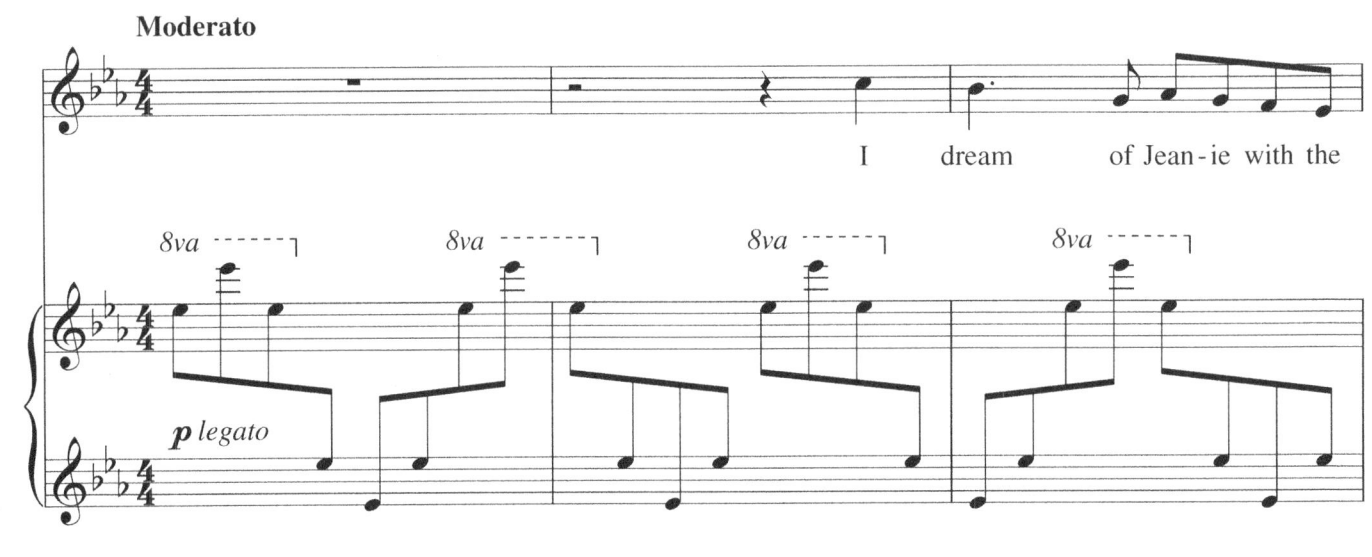

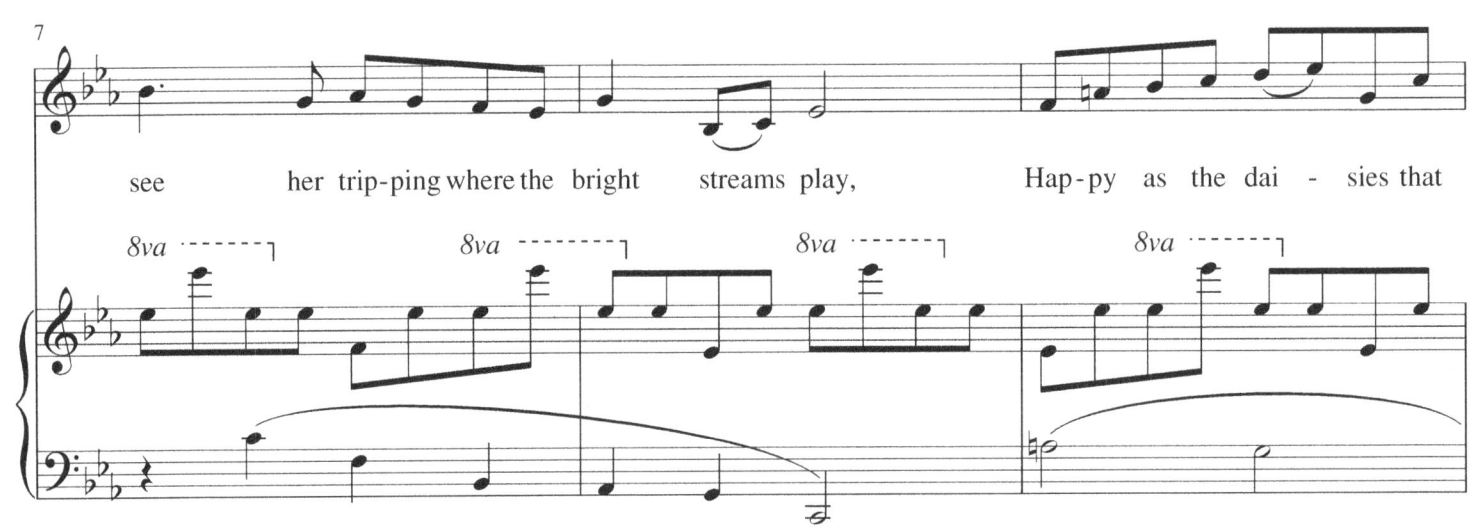

© Copyright 1990 by Boosey & Hawkes, Inc.
New transposition © 2006 by Boosey & Hawkes, Inc.
Copyright for all countries. All rights reserved.

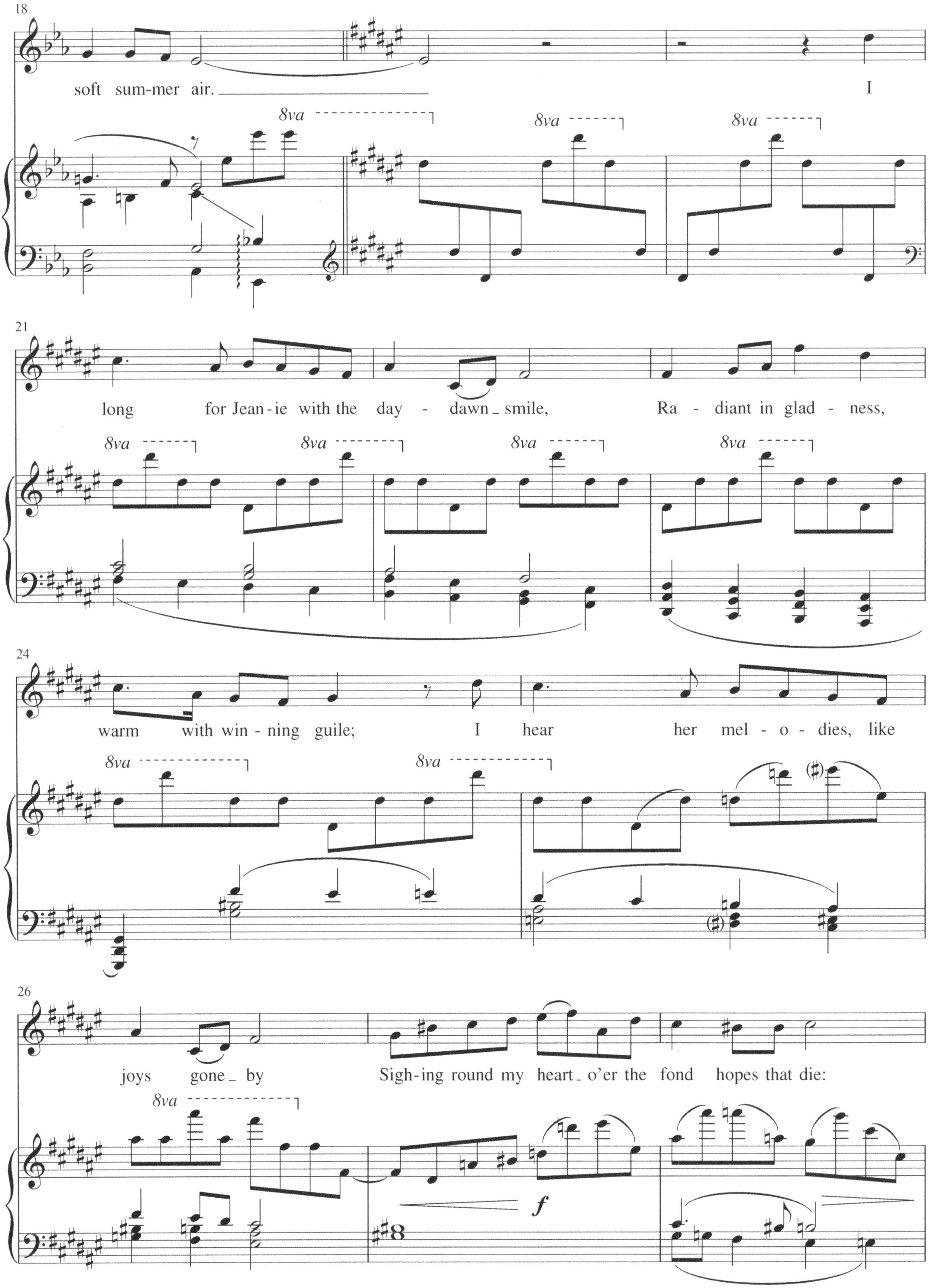
18
soft sum-mer air. I
8va
21
long for Jean-ie with the day - dawn_smile, Ra - diant in glad - ness,
24
warm with win - ning guile; I hear her mel - o - dies, like
26
joys gone_by Sigh-ing round my heart_o'er the fond hopes that die:
f

Nantucket 22-23 May 1982

168

To Shirley Xenia Gabis Rhoads

Love
original key

THOMAS LODGE

NED ROREM

© Copyright 1969 by Boosey & Hawkes, Inc. Copyright Renewed.
Copyright for all countries. All rights reserved.

169

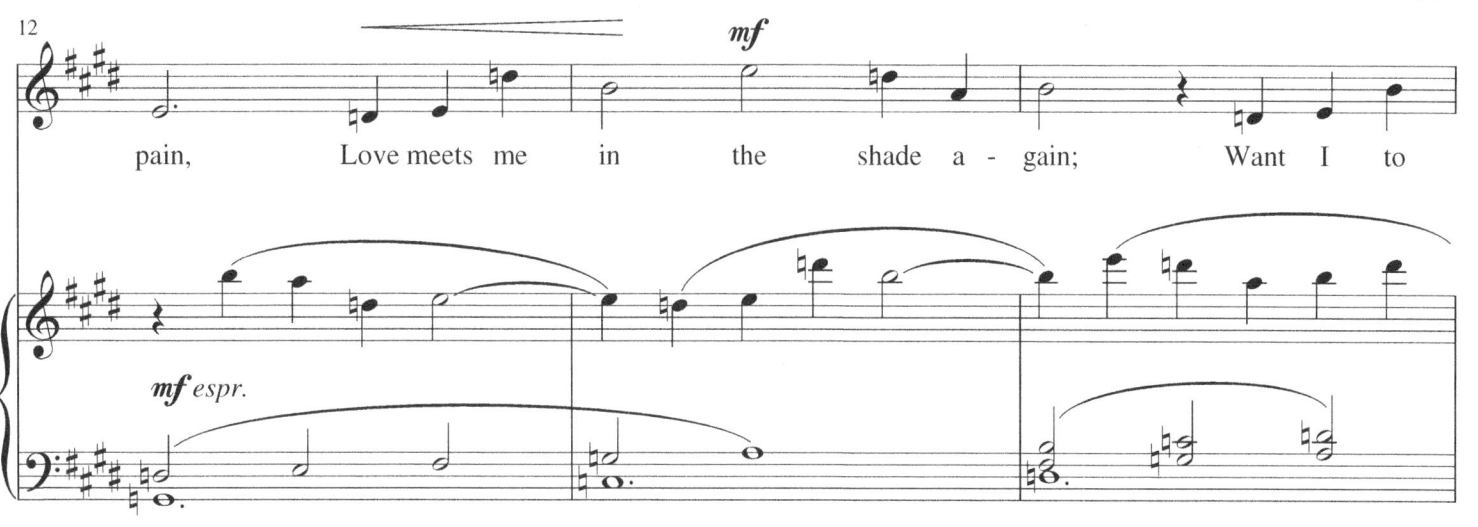

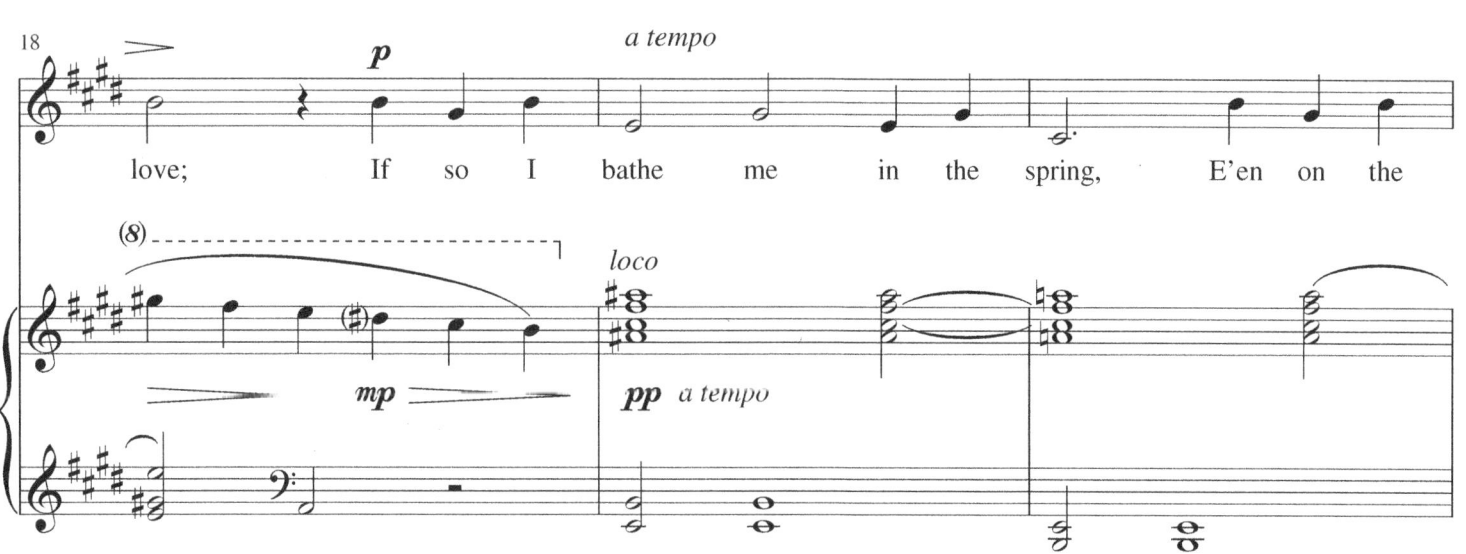

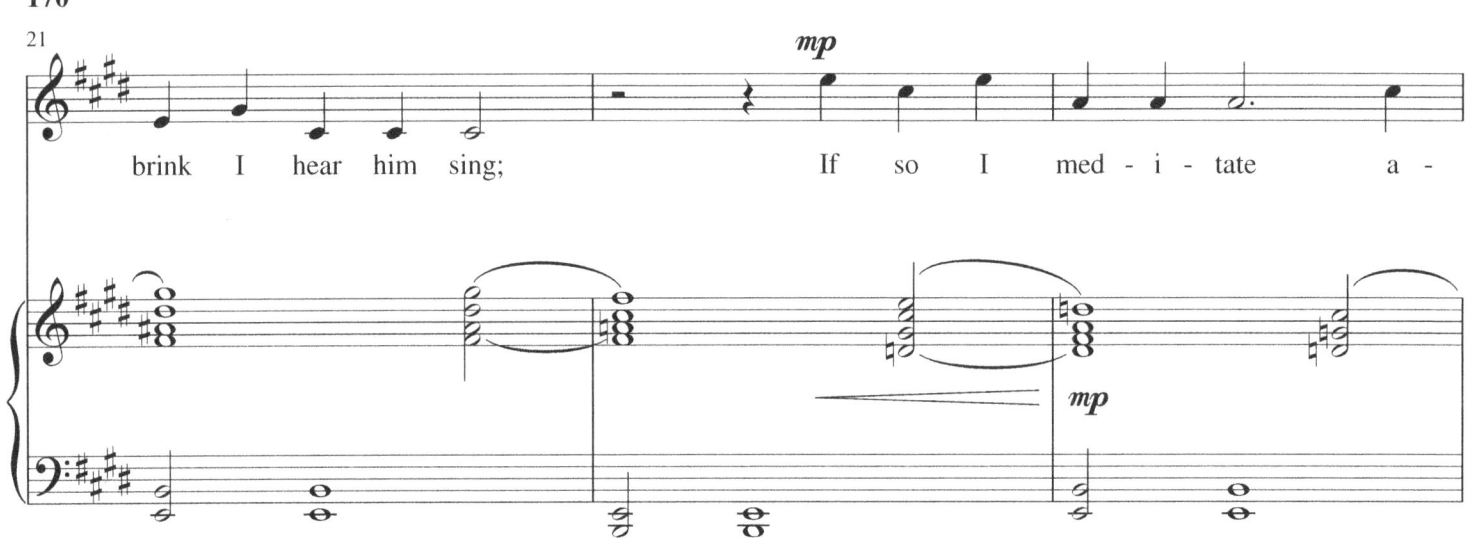

Hyères, 22 July 1953

for my father
Stopping by Woods on a Snowy Evening
original key: E minor

ROBERT FROST

NED ROREM

Andantino (♩ = 56)

p espr.

mp

Whose woods these are I think I know. His house is in the vil-lage though; He will not see me stop-ping here To watch his woods fill up with snow.

mp

rit.

© Copyright 1990 by Boosey & Hawkes, Inc.
New transposition © 2006 by Boosey & Hawkes, Inc.
Copyright for all countries. All rights reserved.
Text from *The Poetry of Robert Frost* edited by Edward Connery Lathem,
© Copyright 1923, 1969 by Holt, Rinehart and Winston. Copyright 1951 by
Robert Frost. Used by permission of Henry Holt and Company, Inc.

Thursday 20 March 1947 N.Y.C.

174

The lads in their hundreds

from *A Shropshire Lad*
original key: A♭ Major

A.E. HOUSMAN
ARTHUR SOMERVELL

Allegretto ma con molto espressione

© Copyright 1904 by Boosey & Co. Ltd.
New transposition © 2006 by Boosey & Hawkes Music Publishers Ltd.

Take, O take those lips away

original key

WILLIAM SHAKESPEARE

PETER WARLOCK

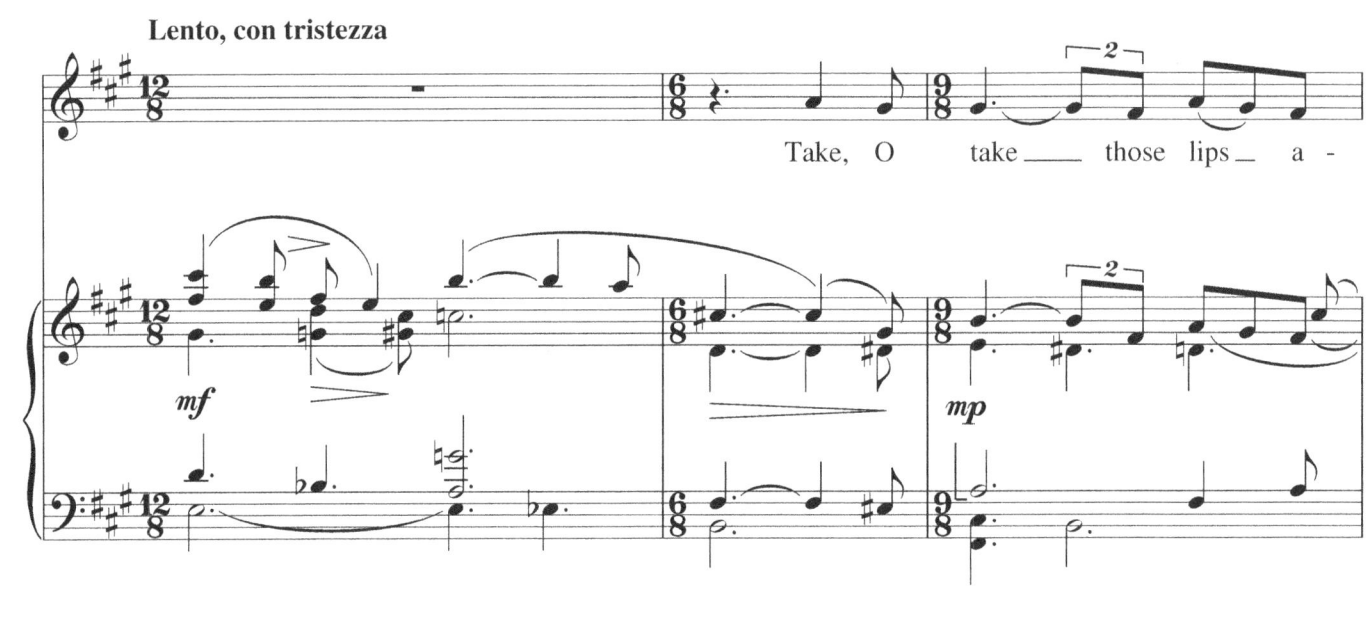

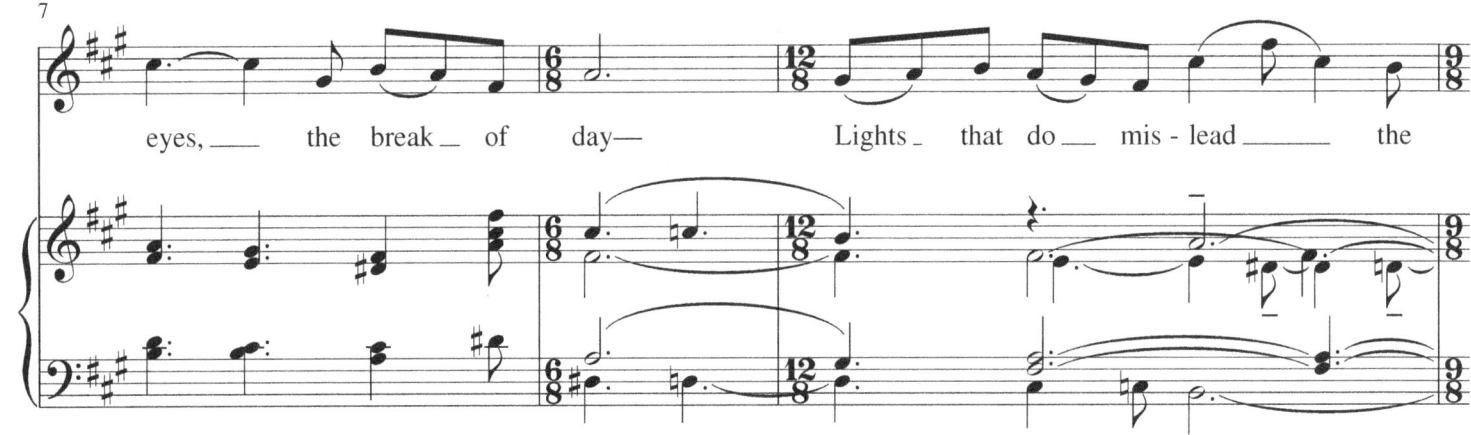

Copyright 1919 by Winthrop Rogers Ltd.
All rights reserved

Bright is the ring of words

from *Songs of Travel*
original key: D Major

ROBERT LOUIS STEVENSON

RALPH VAUGHAN WILLIAMS

© Copyright 1905 by Boosey & Co. Ltd.
New transposition © 2006 by Boosey & Hawkes Music Publishers Ltd.

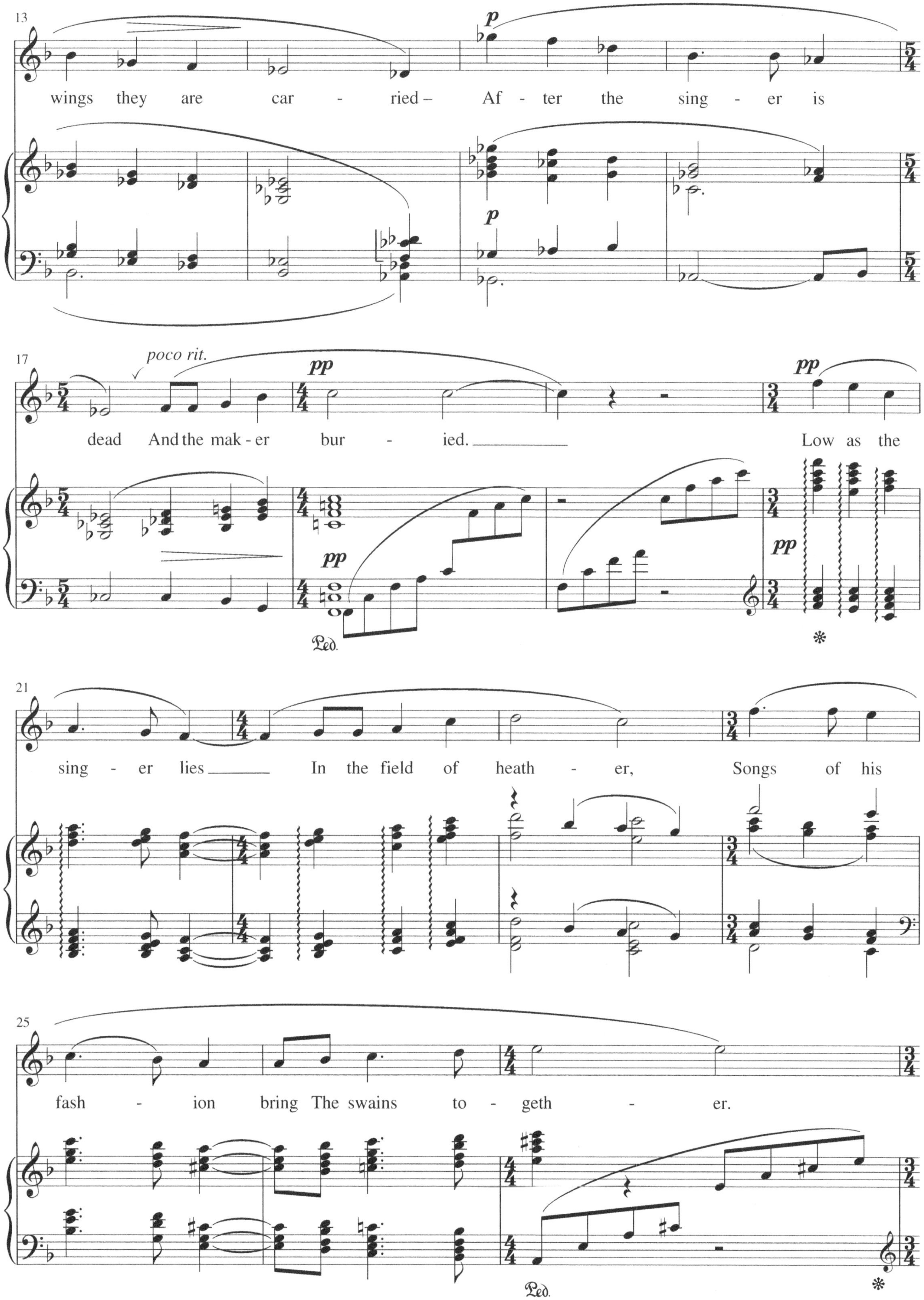
13
p
wings they are car - ried – Af - ter the sing - er is
p
17
poco rit.
pp
dead And the mak - er bur - ied.
pp
Low as the
pp
Ped.
21
sing - er lies In the field of heath - er, Songs of his
25
fash - ion bring The swains to - geth - er.
Ped.

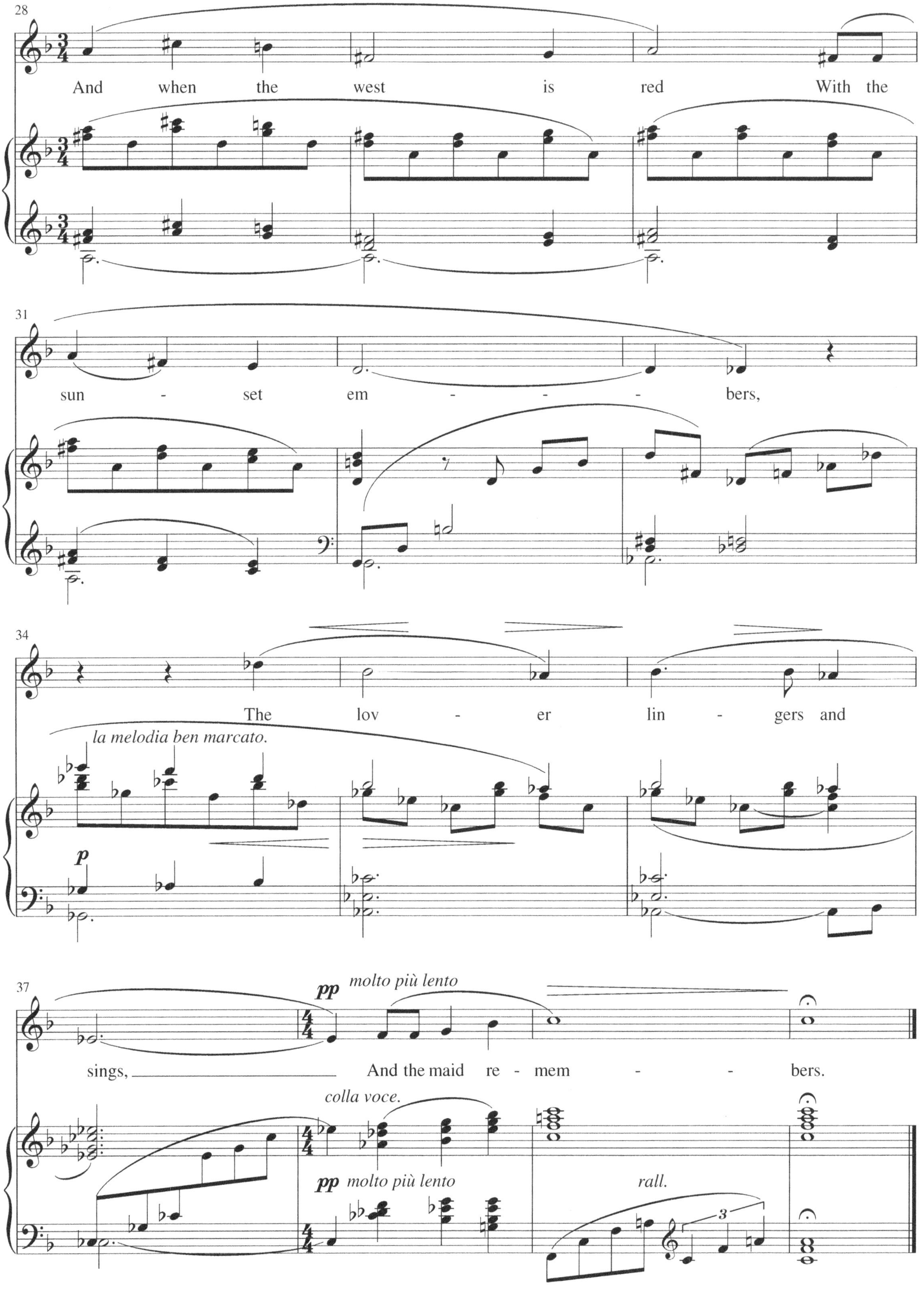
28
And when the west is red With the
31
sun - set em - - - bers,
34
The lov - er lin - gers and
la melodia ben marcato.
p
37
sings, And the maid re - mem - - bers.
pp molto più lento
colla voce.
pp molto più lento
rall.

185

To Mrs. Edmund Fisher

Linden Lea
A Dorset Song

original key: a major 2nd lower

WILLIAM BARNES

RALPH VAUGHAN WILLIAMS

With-in the wood - lands, flow'r-y glad - ed, By the oak trees' moss - y moot; The shin-ing grass blades, tim-ber shad - ed, Now do
(Original) 'Ith - in the wood - lands, flow'r-y glëad - ed, By the woak trees' moss - y moot, The sheen-en grass blëades, tim-ber shëad - ed, Now do

quiv-er un - der foot; And birds do whis - tle o - ver-head, And wa-ter's bub - bling in its
quiv-er un - der voot; An' birds do whis - sle au-ver-head, An' wa-ter's bub - blen in its

© Copyright 1921 by Boosey & Co. Renewed 1939.
New transposition © 2006 by Boosey & Hawkes Music Publishers Ltd.
Copyright for all countries. All rights reserved.

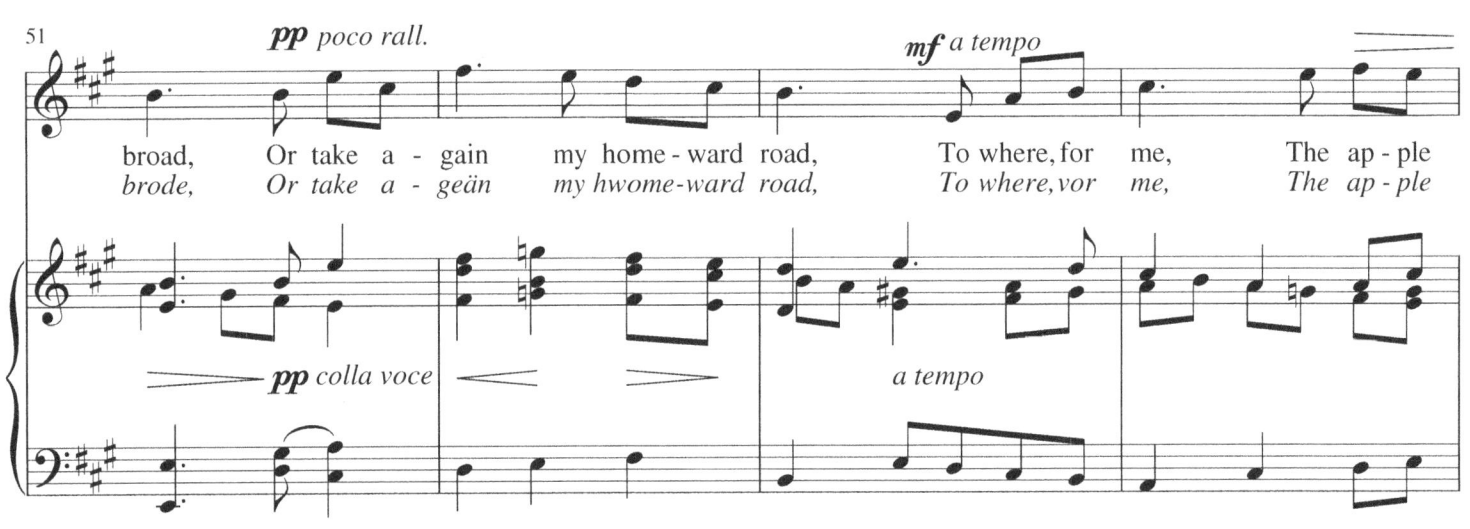